FIELD HOC

Thinking Outside the Box:
Fixing and Enhancing Techniques in Goalkeepers

Erica Crell

Wish Publishing
Terre Haute, Indiana
www.wishpublishing.com

Proofread by MB Ink LLC
Cover designed by Phil Velikan
All photography by Bary Crell, Mobius New Media

Printed in the United States of America
10 9 8 7 6 5 4 3 2 1

Published in the United States by
Wish Publishing
P.O. Box 10337
Terre Haute, IN 47801, USA
www.wishpublishing.com

Distributed in the United States by
Cardinal Publishers Group
www.cardinalpub.com

For Barry, Jordan and Samantha

Table of Contents

Acknowledgments

I would like to extend a big thank you to Widener University for providing the facility for photographs and to Larissa Gillespie and Widener University Field Hockey Coaching Staff for being big supporters. A big thank you to Mikayla Ninos and Colleen Riley for their willingness to model the skills and techniques portrayed in the demonstration photographs. Thank you to Jim Haven for creating the figures of drills. A special thank you to my husband for always supporting everything I do. Without you, my love, none of this would have come to light.

Foreword

Through years of coaching, I have come across many goalkeepers who need little tweaks here and there to get them to a level of play that will make them and their team successful. Sometimes to fix a technique it takes some "out of the box" thinking to make that minor tweak. What I mean is, instead of repeating yourself over and over again that players need to, for instance, "get their weight forward," and drilling them with balls at their feet, sometimes you have to try an alternative. I've found that using things you find around the house or having athletes play another sport will sometimes help remind them to do what you are asking. This book was put together from years of coaching and thinking of drills and approaches that are "outside of the box" for all types of goalkeepers. I have found that I used these ideas more for tweaking skills here and there in college goalkeepers who have been doing the wrong thing their entire high school career, but it can be used for all levels. With a few minor tweaks you can make your goalkeeper more successful with a particular skill. You can use these ideas with any skilled goalkeeper and they do come in handy for those just beginning. Since beginners are fresh to the skill, you can eliminate having to make the corrections later in their career if you implement some of these ideas early on.

Good luck and remember, any idea you have that is "outside the box" is worth a try, at least once, to see if it will work. If it doesn't, there's no shame in trying. If it works, please share with the community — we love new ideas on helping our goalkeepers succeed.

Introduction

Goalkeepers all have their own style. Each one will exhibit some kind of flare to their skills. The important part is that the base technique is consistent across the board for all goalkeepers. I focus on this alot with my goalkeeper, especially emphasizing foot positioning, base position, and weight position. Every coach should focus on these three things if they want to get their goalkeeper to a level of competency. Once you get the base skills down for your goalkeeper, you can then focus on the team or advance individual skills like talking, when to attack or retreat and double-teaming, etc. I get alot of calls from friends who are coaches and they say, "I have this awesome kid who is a great goalkeeper. She has great instincts, but I can't fix this one thing. Can you give me a drill for that?" It doesn't matter if your goalkeeper is in middle school, high school, or college, there is always something that can be worked on. I have come across many things that goalkeepers commonly need to fix. I'm hoping that together we can help each other fix the bad habits with some simple drills and techniques. It will take some hard work and some thinking "outside the box."

Once we have established the basic technique fixes, we can talk more about advanced skill fixes with in-depth drills to help improve the skills and strengths of your goalkeeper and, hopefully the back line of defense. Are you ready to get to work?

chapter 1

Nothing but Weight

When coaches talk about the essentials of kicking, they always mention weight. Not the size or pounds of your goalkeeper, but how your goalkeeper distributes her center of gravity into the movement of a kick. A baseball player will never hit the ball if he's leaning back on his heels. The same concept comes into play for your goalkeeper's movements. You'll hear coaches saying "Get on the balls of your feet" or "Your weight is back." This means that they want the goalkeeper to get her weight more forward and more fluid in her motions. The first thing the goalkeeper should do is get herself back in her basic stance. Have her stay down and in that position when the ball is active and inside her 25-yard line. The basic stance is on the balls of her feet with a little bit of air between her heels and the ground. Her knees should be over her toes and her shoulders and head over her knees. This makes all kicking motions simple and keeps the ball on the ground. If your goalkeeper has all the kicking motions down but the ball is still coming up in the air, you will need to look at her weight. Please keep in mind that the arms and hands do have weight and will affect her center of gravity. Keep an eye on where they are placed. The hand and arm placement should effectively solve the majority of the problems with weight (see the hands section in chapter 2).

Basic Stance

Through the years of coaching, I have noticed that many goalkeepers cannot stay in their basic stance or they think they are in their basic stance but aren't as low as they could get. I try to use a story like this one to emphasize how low their basic stance should be.

"Imagine that you are at a park and you have to go to the little girl's room. You know you can't hold it long enough to get home. But you spy on the far side of the park a big blue box called a 'port-a-pot.' You sigh, but alas, you have to go bad so off you go to the blue box. While inside, you don't want to touch anything so you decide to squat instead of sit." Here they will all giggle, but it gets the point across. At this point, I ask them to imagine that they are in the box and to get in that squat position. Then I go on with the story to explain that there is a bar in front of them, and they decide that they can hold on to it a little bit. From here you will see the hands come forward and into a ready stance position. Then have them adjust their center of gravity so that it is not back but more forward on the balls of their feet while still in the squat position. Remind them that they need to remember this feeling in their hamstrings and calves when they need to be down in the stance. They should be feeling that position every time an active stance is required.

Figure 1: Here is an example of a proper basic stance. Note the hands are in the core position close to the body, the head is over the knees and the knees are over the toes. All weight is forward and feet are shoulder width apart. This will help the goalkeeper have good balance and be able to move into any skill efficiently.

Drills

Drills to work weight distribution can be a little difficult. If your goal-keeper has weight issues, you will need to constantly remind your goal-keeper to lean forward. You may need to get a little more creative in your thinking. Try some thinking "outside the box" for fixing some issues. Like some of the other issues in this book, weight is a hard-to-break habit, and it will take lots of work by you and your goalkeeper to fix. However, you will both be excited by the results when you are finished.

Figure 2: Use this drill to help get the weight in proper position. This drill will help pull the head, shoulders, hands and hips in the correct position. In this "outside the box" thinking drill, I took an old bucket and placed a flat broom inside of it. I weighted that broom down so that it would stay still and thereby created a pole to use in any area. Have a goalkeeper set up to the right or left of the pole. Have her pretend to step to the pole, putting her hands on either side of the pole and her head touching the pole. Work both sides of the goalkeeper. Focus on basic stance, kick movement, and head over the knees while hitting the pole with her head.

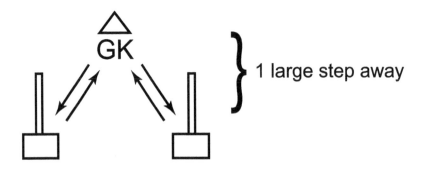

Figure 3: Create 2 poles as shown in Figure 2 and add a cone to form a triangle. They should be a step and a half away from each other. Have you goalkeeper start at the top of the triangle with the cone only. The goalkeeper now opens her hips and steps behind her to the pole. She should be aiming her arms to bisect the pole and her head to hit the pole. Then have her step back to the cone. The goalkeeper then works the other side the same way. Make sure that your goalkeeper stays in her basic stance the entire time throughout her movements. This will eventually work her angles and opening up her hips for kicking and proper movements. Have her work her footwork emphasizing basic stance movement and keeping her weight forward. Work through this for a few minutes each day until you see a change in your goalkeeper's weight distribution.

If you find that your goalkeeper is still not on the balls of her feet, you can try this drill. The air between her heel and the ground doesn't have to be dramatic, but it does have to allow for a little separation between the ground and her heel. You will notice it in her movements if she is not on the balls of her feet. There is an "out of the box" idea for this problem. You can cut a golf ball in half. This is a little higher than what you want for your goalkeeper but it will strengthen the calf muscles and create muscle-motor memory. Now tape each half of the golf ball to the bottom of each shoe at the heel. Have your goalkeeper practice with these on her shoes for a few days. When she takes them off, you will notice some air between her heels and the ground. It may be hard to cut a golf ball so you can use a whole one as well, but do keep in mind that it is rough on the calf muscles and it may cause the ankle to roll.

Another idea is to get a bungee resistance help cord from your track coach. Strap up your goalkeeper with this bungee cord and have her move around the cage with you pulling her forward. You can also advance this drill by having your goalkeeper stand in position. Have balls rolled at her gradually and then shot at your goalkeeper. As she moves through her kick, pull the cord thereby pulling your goalkeeper forward. Work on this for a few weeks and you will see an improvement in weight distribution.

chapter 2

Fix the Kick

Have you looked at your goalkeeper and said "Something is wrong with her kick"? Well it can be fixed with some hard work and some "outside the box" thinking. Take a close look at the kick. What part of the kick has the problem? You may have to film it and place it side by side with another goalkeeper to figure out exactly what it is that needs to be fixed. Maybe all of it, maybe just a part of it — you won't know until you break it down and take a closer look.

Hands

I find that in most instances, it has to do with where the hands are placed. Believe it or not, the hands have an impact on weight. Why? Well, stand in a goalkeeper stance. Go ahead, I'll wait. Now shift your arms directly behind you. Do you feel yourself being pulled back a little? Now shift your arms directly forward in front of you. Do you feel the difference? This is important to note. When you watch most goalkeepers they pull one hand back on their kicks. I think they believe that it helps give them power like it does for kicking a soccer ball. But in reality, it does far worse. It pulls their weight back and does take away from some of the power and accuracy of the kick. Think about most sports that focus on propelling a ball forward. Baseball pitchers are a good example. The pitcher throws his arm forward and almost points to where the ball is going. When he finishes, both hands are forward and ready for the ball to come back at him.

When a goalkeeper pulls one of her arms back on a kick, she is pulling her weight back a little, thereby forcing the ball in the air and taking some power off the ball. This can be very dangerous and create alot of corners for your team. So the first thing you need to focus on when fixing your goalkeeper's kicks is her hands. Where are they positioned when kicking? Where should they be?

Solution

I tell my goalkeeper to bring her hands together and point to where she wants the ball to go. By forcing her hands to point, she is now pulling all her weight forward. In addition, by pointing to where she wants the ball to go, the goalkeeper is now turning her hips and, in turn, hopefully her foot to the direction she wants the ball to go. It seems simple, but try getting your goalkeeper to do it. First, she has to get over the silliness feeling. Then you need to get her to remember to do it and in one smooth motion. You might giggle a little when teaching her because you will see some goalkeepers start with kicking the ball and then moving their hands to where the ball is going after kicking the ball. I sometimes tell them that they are escorting the ball to the place they want it to go with their hands. I make them actually say "Go there ball" or "Here you go ball" while they point. I know it seems silly, but I have found that it has worked.

Drills

Here are some simple drills for this problem.

Figure 4: Example of a simple drill that can be done to work on the hands. Have your goalkeepers kick between themselves. They will need to work on accuracy and speed here. As they kick they should be pointing to their target. If you don't have two goalkeepers, you can have your goalkeeper kick to the backstop of the cage, focusing on her hands. Notice how dramatic their hands are in the point.

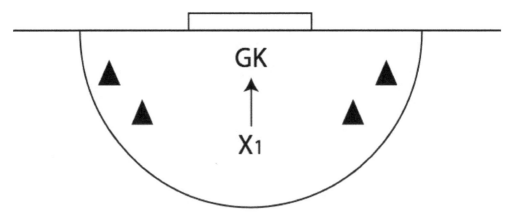

Figure 5: Example of another simple drill that works accuracy and hands. Have your goalkeeper work on aiming rolled or hit balls to specific gates for targets. You do not need to do this in the circle. You can do this in any space. It's just for accuracy and working the hands.

Once your goalkeeper understands the concept of the hands moving forward, you will need to create a muscle-motor memory for this skill. Here's where thinking "outside the box" comes in handy. You will need to get an elastic band for your goalkeepers. You can purchase one at any sporting goods store or your athletic trainer may have one you can borrow. It should not be too restricting. Wrap this band around her hands just past the gloves. It should be somewhat loose so that she can pull her hands apart to get up out of a dive or pull apart for a slide tackle. I use the bands made for leg stretches that you pull apart for Pilates. Make your goalkeeper wear this for practices for a few weeks. Besides reminding her to keep her hands together by basically pulling the hands together and in front of her, it will strengthen the arms a little, too. Test the skill about a week after putting the strap on by removing it and hitting some balls to your goalkeeper for her to kick to a target. If you see the hands staying in front, she won't need to wear it until you see the issue come back. If she still is leaning a little, put the band back on. I've had goalkeepers of all levels, and I've made them all wear the band at some point in their careers. It works and it is the most widely used piece in my "outside the box" drills.

Now, we don't want your goalkeeper to be pointing or talking to the ball when it comes to game time. So you will have to phase these things out as you notice the hands comfortably moving forward on the kick. I have found that over time goalkeepers adopt their own style to this motion and just keep their hands at hip length and move them slightly forward.

Figure 6: An example of a strap in use.

Figure 6 (continued): An example of a strap in use.

Each goalkeeper will be different in the look, but the base idea needs to be there (the hands coming forward to the ball and not away). I really enjoy watching the progressions of this with my goalkeeper. I find that once I get her hands accustomed to moving forward, I see more power and more consistency with the ball staying low on the ground, as well as greater accuracy delivering the ball where she wants it to go.

Figure 7: An example of a goalkeeper moving her hands along hip level during a kick.

Hips

Another issue with the kick could be the hips. Once you have gotten the hands moving the correct way to keep the weight forward, you will need to take a look at the hips. Sometimes, a goalkeeper will be able to move her hands in the direction of the ball, but she doesn't pull the hips and head over to where she sent the ball. Not moving the hips will cause problems when the ball comes at her faster. When it comes at her faster, she will need to open her hips for a quick send back out. If she doesn't open her hips correctly, the ball will go directly back to the shooter and up the middle of the circle. For a goalkeeper to be successful, she will need to send the balls out to Zone 3 or the lowest angle from where she is standing. If you don't know about zones then you need to start by reading *Mastering the Net: Field Hockey Goalkeeping Basics*. She can't send the ball to Zone 3 unless she opens her hips.

Figure 8:
A) An example of a goalkeeper who isn't opening her hips during the kick.
B) An example of a goalkeeper who is opening her hips during the kick.

The hips are trickier to teach muscle-motor memory because every goal-keeper has a different type of flexibility. Some will need to really focus on opening the hips and turning the foot; others will have no problem. I created a small footwork drill to correct this problem. You will need your goalkeeper to do this at home as well as at practice. Have her stand square to the ball and then pretend she is kicking it to her side. Place a pole (from figure 2) right where she would kick the ball. You will need your goalkeeper to then step into the pole. Have her place her foot so that it is almost kicking the pole. Her hands will go on either side of the pole, and her head must connect with the pole. Obviously we want the head to do this lightly, and your goalkeeper should have a helmet on.

Figure 9: This drill will help pull the hips in the correct position. Use the bucket pole from Figure 2 and have your goalkeeper pretend to step to the pole, putting her hands on either side of the pole and her head touching the pole. Have her foot kicking the bucket so that her hips are turning. Work both sides of the goalkeeper.

With a drill like this, your goalkeeper is now learning to bring the hands through with the hips turning. The foot is in the correct position and her head will now be over her foot. Her hands will be on either side of the pole thereby bisecting her leg as well. Because the hands moved, the shoulders turned and shifted too. Your goalkeeper should work both sides and do this about 5 minutes a day or so. As she starts to look better at this drill, you can then start adding a live ball that she needs to come in contact with. Just move the pole slightly farther away from your goal-keeper. It will take some time to get your goalkeeper to get this motion into memory. I'd work on this for several weeks.

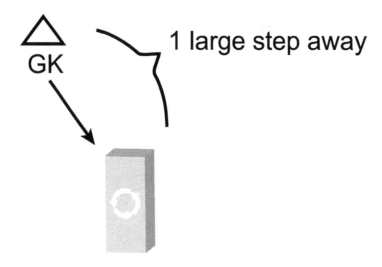

Figure 10: Have your goalkeeper stand at a cone and place a small trashcan (about as high as her hips – I like the thin blue recycle cans) slightly behind the goalkeeper. Have your goalkeeper drop step and turn her body to the trashcan. While doing so she is to smack the trash can on either side with her stick and glove. If the trashcan is small and light enough, you can even ask her to pick it up slightly. When she is done, she will step back to center at the cone. Work both sides of the goalkeeper. Do each side for 1 minute.

Foot Position — Kicking Motion

When your goalkeeper kicks, does the ball pop up? If so, there can be three reasons for this: placement of where the ball meets the foot, how the foot is positioned or where her weight is distributed. We focused on weight earlier. Let's take a look at foot position. Feet placement is an essential part of goalkeeping, and if your goalkeeper doesn't have kicking down, you will have some problems getting the ball out of the circle. I often videotape my goalkeeper's feet from the ground. The reason for this is that most goalkeepers pick up their feet on their kicks. They don't even know they do it. When you videotape from the ground, you will be able to see if a goalkeeper does this. It is essential that you have her keep her feet on the ground, almost wiping the bottom of her foot on the ground as she moves into the kicking position. I tell my goalkeeper it's like swishing a bug and trying to get it off the bottom of your foot except instead of pulling away from the bug you are pushing to it. Have your goalkeeper keep constant contact with the ground in her movements for the kick. We don't want her to stomp or swing at the ball in her kicks.

Figure 11: An example of a proper kicking broken down into phases.

Figure 12: An example of incorrect kicking broken down into phases.

To solve foot placement problems, it will take some hard work on the goalkeeper's part. First, you will need to show her what you see. Then have her kick smoothly almost wiping her feet on the ground. Please make sure she is not doing a swinging or stomping motion.

Figure 13: An example of incorrectly swinging the leg to kick.

Figure 14: An example of an incorrect kicking motion of stomping the foot at the ball.

Solution

Start with your goalkeeper's feet parallel to each other in the basic stance. If you don't know about this then you need to start by reading *Mastering the Net*. As the ball moves to your goalkeeper's personal space on the right or left foot, have your goalkeeper move her foot forward so that she meets the ball out in front of her body in a small motion. Again, she should use a wiping-a-bug-off-your-foot motion against the ground. The foot and hips should open up, pointing to where the goalkeeper wants the ball to go. Then, as she makes contact with the ball, the hands and head should be over the ball and pointing to where she wants the ball to go.

Figure 15: An example of a proper basic stance.

Figure 16: An example of a proper hand and foot placement.

Drill

Here is a circuit drill that you can do with your goalkeeper to work on the feet. It's probably a good idea to film this from the feet up so that you can see the progress. This is something that should be done to start each practice until your goalkeeper has perfected this movement.

A)

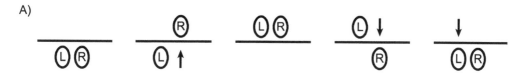

Figure 17:
A: Start first with your goalkeeper standing behind the end-line. Have her move her right foot over the line, then her left foot over the line, now back over the line with her right foot and then her left. Have her do this continuously in her basic stance for 20 seconds. Make sure she has all her coordination intact while doing this. Hands should be moving forward and it might be good to have the band on her if she has a problem with moving backward.

B)

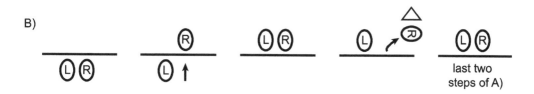

B: Now have your goalkeeper move down the line to the next station. She will start the same way she did in figure A. But when she steps forward with her right and then left foot, she then will move into a kick position with her right foot. Then back to basic stance and back over the line again. Do this continuously for 20 seconds. This will be a little slower than in figure A to get the proper foot positioning down. Then work the left foot kick doing the same thing as the right.

C)

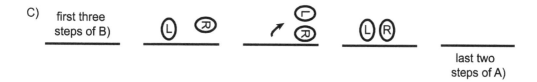

C: Again, have your goalkeeper move down the line to the next station and set up just like in figures A and B. She will do the same as in figure B but as the right foot moves into position to kick, the left foot comes for a follow-through. Then retreat back over the line to do it again. Do this for 20 seconds continuously. Again, this will move slower than in figure A because of the movements and you want your goalkeeper to focus on her kick and follow-through movement. Then work the left foot kick doing the same thing as the right.

D)

First three
steps of B)

last two
steps of A)

D: In the last time through, your goalkeeper will now move down the line again to the next station and set up like the others. A ball will be rolled to her and she will step over the line to clear and follow through. Don't worry about where it is going right now although if it's done right it should come off the foot on a 45 degree angle. Work just the right foot and then the left. Do this again for 20 seconds. As the goalkeeper gets more advanced with this and more comfortable in her movement you can alternate or do whichever foot you'd like in an equal amount to each side. Just make sure that she is focusing on her positioning. Make sure that you do this for both sides of your goalkeeper.

Foot Position — Where on the Foot

The point of the kick is to gain momentum and send the ball back out at the same speed or faster than it came in to your goalkeeper. This can only be achieved if your goalkeeper perfects her kicking skill. It's important that the ball is sent out, not only fast, but in an accurate location. This is why where the ball strikes the foot is just as important as how the foot is positioned. Your goalkeeper should focus to make contact with the ball in the middle of the foot in the instep or arch area of the foot. This allows for the best accuracy and control. Try using figure 20 to help with this, as well as making your goalkeeper kick at target cones in the correct placement on the field.

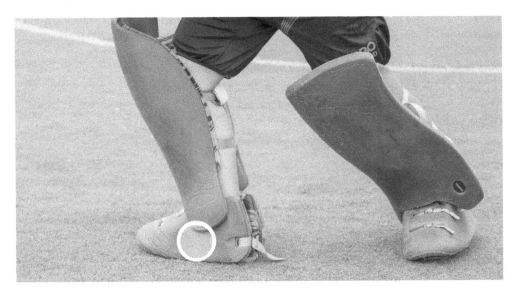

Figure 18: An example of where the ball should strike the foot.

To accurately send the ball out of the circle in the area your goalkeeper wants it to go, she will need to position her foot, hips, shoulders, and head in that direction as well. This is why the hands are so important: they pull the hips and shoulders into the position and direction of the ball.

Figure 19: An example of a proper kick.

Drill

Try these drills to help put the kicking motions together. If you find that your goalkeeper is kicking with the toe or heel, you will need to work some of these drills.

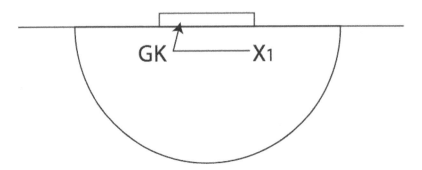

Figure 20: This drill is simple and can be done with another goalkeeper or an assistant. Have the goalkeeper stand sideways to the goal at one post. Have an assistant or another goalkeeper stand just past the opposite post. Have the two face each other. The assistant will push balls to the goalkeeper's goal-side foot. The goalkeeper will send the balls into the cage. This drill has the goalkeeper focusing on all the things that she has been taught to correct her kick. Filming this once in a while will help you to identify what needs more tweaking.

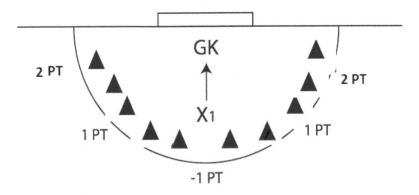

Figure 21: This simple drill works on where the ball should strike the foot. If done properly the ball should hit the target. Put the gates at the 35 degree angle of the circle or below (zones 2 and 3). A variation of this is to have several gates at different angles to the goalkeeper and give points based on which gate is hit. Higher points should be given for the gates on the lower angles.

Non-kicking Foot

While we are on the feet, let's take a look at the non-kicking foot. As the kicking foot does its motion talked about in *Mastering the Net* and in the previous scenarios, the non-kicking foot should be still. Sometimes goalkeepers turn their non-kicking foot and body to make a kick. As is the concept in many ball sports, you want to face the ball as it approaches you. If a baseball player were to turn his body before catching a ground ball and that ball takes a hop, then most likely he will be off balance and in the incorrect position to play the ball. Not to mention the fact that he will now not be set up to send the ball to the player he wants, should he catch it. The same concept applies here. The placement of the non-kicking foot is just as important as the kicking foot. Again, you should videotape your goalkeeper's kicks. You will see if the non-kicking foot moves or not. I have noticed that younger goalkeepers move the foot to set themselves up to send the ball to the correct place. This becomes a habit that carries through their careers. As they get older, you may only see it for slower-paced balls, but it's there and it's a bad habit that will inhibit the hips, hands, and shoulder movement. I also see more of a swinging motion with the kicking foot when the non-kicking foot turns. Figure 22 shows the non-kicking foot turning incorrectly to prepare for an incoming ball. Figure 23 shows the proper position of the non-kicking foot.

Figure 22: An example of a non-kicking foot turning to receive a ball to the kicking foot. We should not see this happen in our goalkeepers kicking motion.

Figure 23: An example of a non-kicking foot in the proper position so that the kicking foot can play a ball.

Drills

I have found several things that come in handy to try to fix this habit. Some of these "out of the box" ideas will require some help from other goalkeepers or another coach. Also, like some of my other drills, it will require some work for your goalkeeper to do at home as well.

Figure 24: In this example, you will need to put a string out on the outside of the non-kicking foot, so that the goalkeeper can focus on keeping the foot on the string. Balls should be rolled to the goalkeeper's kicking foot. As the goalkeeper gets better at focusing on the non-kicking foot and kicking properly, speed up the balls and start hitting them. Keep advancing through this drill working both sides of the goalkeeper until you feel the goalkeeper is comfortable enough to remove the string and continue to kick properly.

Another way to keep the non-kicking foot still is to start with rolled balls and work your way up to hitting at the goalkeeper. Focus on her keeping her non-kicking foot still. No follow through is allowed. She is to only reach into the kick and hold the position. Keep working this on both sides of the goalkeeper. You can also use the drill in figure 17 to help with this motion.

Figure 25: Use a spare goalkeeper or an assistant coach to step on the non-kicking foot to keep it still during the kick. You will want to release the foot just after the kick so that the goalkeeper can then do a follow-through. Again, you will want to start with rolled balls first and then work your way up to hitting the ball. Eventually, you should add targets for where you want the ball to go. Be sure to work both sides of your goalkeeper.

The Stick and the Kick

Nothing infuriates me more than when I see a goalkeeper reach for a ball with her stick when she could have used her feet. This hinders the point of being a goalkeeper. Try to emphasize to your goalkeeper that the stick is an extension of the arm and shouldn't be used where her feet can. I find a lot of it has to do with laziness. Make your goalkeeper move to get the ball. This means actually shuffling, lunging or sprinting to the ball. By using her feet, your goalkeeper is using a larger surface area to cover the goalmouth. If she uses her stick for situations where a foot can be used, she is significantly decreasing that surface area for saving the goal and covering the goalmouth. There are two ways you can help a goalkeeper to get this habit to disappear. The first, my most popular way, is to take away the stick. Make her practice for a day or two without it. Trust me, she will feel naked and it hinders her from other skills in which she will need the stick. She will quickly learn to get her feet there to stop a ball. The other "out of the box" idea is to replace the stick with a pool noodle. It gives her that sense that there is something there in her hand, but it's useless against a field hockey ball. Again, I would do this for a whole practice or maybe even two. Both of these have been successful at changing the thought pattern and getting the feet to move to the ball instead of reaching with the stick.

Figure 26: An example of a goalkeeper playing without a stick.

chapter 3

Angles
Working the Goalkeeper's Circle Area to the Fullest

Although, some coaches may say that kicking is the most important skill — believe it or not, angles are the most important and the first thing that goalkeepers should learn. It is actually a difficult concept to teach and learn. Every coach teaches it differently, and I find that I sometimes have to teach it differently depending on my goalkeeper. The reason why I stress the importance of angles is that your goalkeeper can have a beautiful kick, but if she isn't in the correct place in the circle, she won't be able to use that kick. Sometimes even the worst goalkeepers look decent just by being in the right place at the right time. The shooting and cage angles can make or break a goalkeeper's career. So the first thing you need to do is figure out what angle concept your goalkeeper will understand. See *Mastering the Net* for information on angles.

Drills

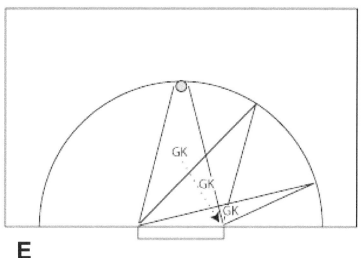

Figure 27: Use this drill to work your goalkeeper's angles so that they understand. Get a long piece of string and attach one end to the bottom of the cage on one post and the other end to the other post at the bottom. Pull the string out to the top of the circle. This is now the triangle shooting angle. You will need to tell the goalkeeper to position themselves in their normal position in basic stance. Replace them and have them stand at the tip of the string at the top of the circle to see what you just saw from there. From here have them position you to where they think they should have been positioned. Ask them if the cage can be covered with one step, two steps, etc.? They need to understand how they can position themselves to cover the cage with one step to either side to prevent a goal. Move the string around the circle doing the same thing. They should notice how the triangle shooting angle gets smaller the lower you go down the circle. Have them move in the proper positions according to the cage and the triangle shooting angle. Make sure they are moving along this angle in the proper movements in their triangle. See **Mastering the Net** *for proper movements around the cage.*

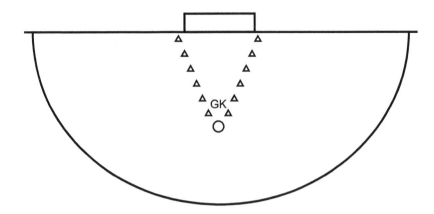

Figure 28: Use this drill to work the goalkeepers angles so that they understand movement within the triangle shooting angle. Set up cones from the post to the stroke making a triangle. This is the movement and location they need to be in to cover the triangle shooting angles properly. They should notice how high they need to be for a ball that is at the top of the circle and how close to the post they need to be for a ball that is at the end of the circle. You can also use this in conjunction with figure 27 too so that they understand the two.

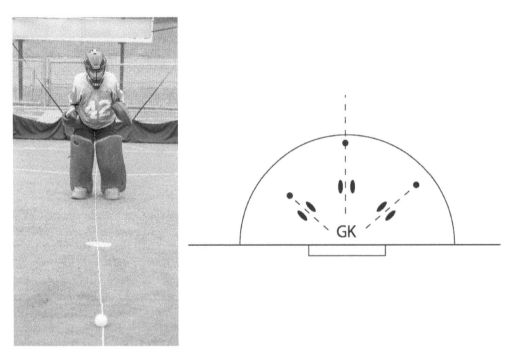

Figure 29: If the string concept doesn't work in the triangle form, you can try a singular string. Attach the string to the dead center of the cage at the bottom, pull the string all the way up to the top of the circle and have the ball at the top of the circle. Now have your goalkeeper straddle the string in her proper position in the circle. This is another way to teach angles. Move the string and ball around the circle and have the goalkeeper move with the string in the proper movements to cover the shooting angle. You can use this in conjunction with figure 28 too.

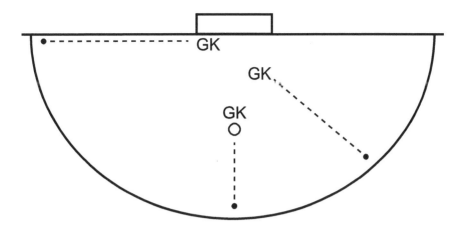

Figure 30: This shows how the goalkeeper can cover the goal and stay on the proper angle when the ball is at different positions around the circle.

Proper Movement

The point of proper movement in the circle is to protect the goal and make sure that it is always covered with at least one movement. Remind your goalkeeper to keep her movements short, but explosive. A triangle is a part of her movement angles. Goalkeepers want to stay within this triangle to be on angle (see figure 32). Do not let your goalkeeper round out her angle to the ball or her angle will be unaligned. Instead, have her open her hips and point her toes to the goal post or stroke mark and then square out. As the ball moves faster, she will need to shuffle or turn and sprint, then square out. For a beginner, move slowly through this process. First, start with opening her hips and facing the ball, then progress to the turn and sprint. Remind your goalkeeper to stay low when opening her hips, and her height should not change. Do not let her "pop up." Slight movement in her height as she moves along her angle will decrease her speed in moving through these movements.

Have her maintain the ready position when she begins to advance off of the goal-line toward an attacker. As the distance to the ball decreases, your goalkeeper should begin to break her body movement down by shifting into smaller movements known as the "cha-cha-cha". (see *Mastering the Net* to understand footwork and the cha-cha-cha). Your goalkeeper is then able to maintain balance and body control.

Figure 31: All movements should be done in basic stance, on the balls of her feet with her weight forward, remaining at the same level through all movements and while changing direction. When moving along the angle, the goalkeeper opens her hips, turns her shoulders, and points her toe back to the post. As you notice here in figure A, the white line illustrates that the goalkeeper's head remains at the same level as she moves through the angle. She remains in her basic stance through her movement. In figure B you see the difference in height of the goalkeeper's head. By relaxing her body on her turn, she transitions out of her basic stance and is now standing upright. Here you see what happens if she pops her head up during her turn. By doing this, she is now losing seconds in the turn and is not preparing her body for the next play or skill that needs to be performed. Make sure that your goalkeeper stays level and in her basic stance through all movements around the goal.

Solution

Goalkeepers sometimes rush this movement and either don't break down their steps or don't open up their hips. Let's first start with the sprint and breakdown, or "cha cha cha." As your goalkeeper is advancing to an attacker in a sprint, she will need to slow herself down. She must break these large sprint steps into much smaller, controlled steps so that she can prepare to perform a skill on the attacker. These are three to four steps that are smaller and controlled. It helps to have your goalkeeper recite "cha-cha-cha" as she runs through a drill and breaks down. It is one step forward that is smaller from the previous step; the next with the other foot will be smaller yet; and the third and possibly fourth with the original foot will bring her back to the basic stance and still position, ready to perform a skill on the attacker. This should be a smooth motion and not even a second thought in your goalkeepers mind, once she understands it.

Drill

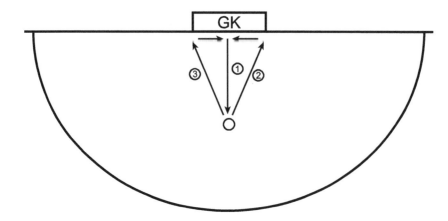

Figure 32: In this drill you can see how a goalkeeper can practice her movements around the cage. She starts in the center of the cage and 1. sprints up to the stroke mark. She must breakdown her steps just before the stroke mark. When she stops at the stroke mark she then points her left toe back to the left post behind her. Make sure that your goalkeeper is level here. In addition, not only should her toe point but her hips should turn, her shoulders should turn and she should be pointing back to the post. 2. She then sprints to the post and just before reaching it turns her body to face out to the field. It is important here that you have your goalkeeper imagine that there is a ball outside the circle moving down the field to the end-line. Have her looking out to the field on her run and not back at the post. Have her stop at the post facing the field and parallel to the end-line. Her hip and pads should be against the post. Now have your goalkeeper drop her right foot across the goalmouth and turn her body facing the center of the field. She then will shuffle back to the center of the goal. 1. She starts the sprint to the stroke mark again. But this time she points her right toe back to the post behind her. Make sure that your goalkeeper is level here. 3. She then sprints to the post. "Again, have your goalkeeper imagine that there is a ball outside the circle moving down the field to the endline. Have her looking out to the field on her run and not back at the post. This time she will drop her left foot and shuffle along the goalmouth to the center of the cage. The last part of this drill is to have your goalkeeper 1. sprint up to the stroke and breakdown. You can change this drill a little by having them shuffle instead of sprint to the post. Both will be used in a game. It is important to note that the eyes need to be out facing the field. I do this drill everyday with my goalkeeper so it becomes a muscle-motor memory for them.

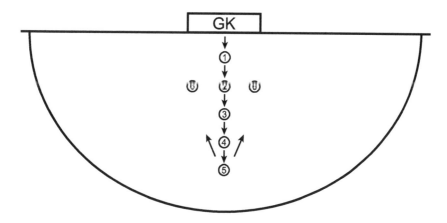

Figure 33: This is a breakdown drill of figure 32. Start with your goalkeeper on the goalmouth in the center of the cage. Have her sprint up to each cone and breakdown. Make your goalkeeper say "cha-cha-cha" as she is breaking down. At cone 5 have her turn and sprint to cone 6. Repeat this process over and over again until they understand breaking down.

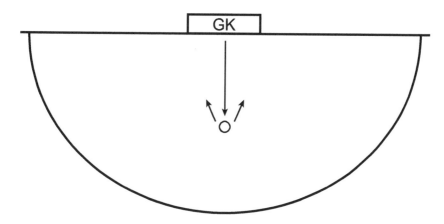

Figure 34: This is another breakdown of figure 32. Have your goalkeeper start the drill on the goalmouth and sprint up to the stroke and breakdown. Have them pause at the breakdown. Have her point her toe back to the post but not go. From here make the adjustments that need to be made. I often have to remind them to turn the shoulders, hands and head along with the hip and foot. Once you have them in the correct position, let them go through the drill. From here, your goalkeeper will start the process all over again but working the other side. Do this several times with your goalkeeper until they get the idea that the whole body needs to turn to make a straight line back to the post.

Once your goalkeeper understands the breakdown footwork, you will need to work on the hips turning and the movement. From the stroke mark, your goalkeeper will need to open her hips and point her toe directly back to the post she wants to go to. I cannot emphasize enough how important the hands are for this movement. Your goalkeeper needs to bring her hands over to point as well. By doing so, the shoulders and head turn to the proper position.

I have noticed that some goalkeepers turn their non-lead foot on this pivot. This foot needs to stay put and the hips need to open up. Pay close attention to the feet of your goalkeeper as she runs through her movements around the cage. Some minor tweaks and you can improve and gain speed on your goalkeeper's movements.

Drill

The "outside the box" thinking for this is a little simple. Have your goalkeeper break down at the top of the stroke and you, as the coach, step on her non-lead foot. From here, have her go into her pivot movement while you are stepping on her non-lead foot. You will need to work this for a few weeks to get your goalkeeper to have muscle-motor memory for this.

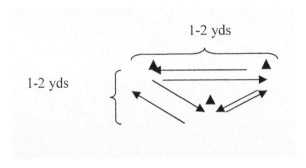

Figure 35: This is a variation of Figure 3. Put 3 cones in a triangle about a lunge width away from each other. Have your goalkeeper start at the top cone and open her right hip and point back to the bottom right cone. Then back up the top cone again. From here she will use the opposite foot and point back and down to the left cone. Then back up to the top cone again. Repeat this for 2 minutes working on pointing the toe back and turning the foot, hip, shoulders, hands, and head.

Also try to use some of the drills from previous chapters, particularly figures 2, 3, 9 and 10.

After showing your goalkeeper the angles concept and the proper movement in her area, you will want to drill it into her memory. The majority of goals scored are because the goalkeeper got beat and was out of position to play the ball successfully. A goalkeeper should always know where she is in relation to the goal. Then, she will be able to know if a shot is wide without having to look behind her for reference. She must be able to mentally draw lines from the ball to the posts and bisect the middle of the angle (meaning positioning between the imaginary lines that are drawn from the two posts to the ball) (see the angles chapter in *Mastering the Net*). Make sure that your goalkeeper is playing the ball, not the attacker. She must be able to see that she has to play directly behind the ball in relation to the goal. Angles take constant work and practice, as well as reinforcement by the coach. It seems silly, but I make my goalkeeper run her angles blindfolded. I tell her that she should know that space like the back of her hand and be able to feel her domain by the steps she takes without having to glance backward. I also show her clues that she can use on the field in front of her to help her know where she is on her angle (e.g., light posts, field signs, field lines, cage across the other end of the field).

Drills

Some of these drills should help with angle movement.

Place a blind fold over the goalkeeper's eyes so that she cannot see. Place her in the center of the cage, facing the stroke mark, and on the endline. When you say go, she should be able to know exactly how many steps its takes her to get to the stroke mark. From here she will run through the drill from figure 32. She should break down her steps and run through the drill smoothly. Your goalkeeper may get a little hesitant and slow down a little when she knows the post is coming, so you can help her verbally with this but she should be on the money when she extends her arms to find the post. If she can't run through this drill smoothly, you will need to do more of figure 32 to really create a muscle-motor memory for her. The purpose for this is for her to realize that she needs to be so intune with the circle that she doesn't need to keep turning her head to look for the post or use her stick to find the cage.

Another drill for understanding movement in the circle requires using a soccer ball. Stand at the top of the circle, bouncing the ball. Have your goalkeeper blindfolded and in the proper goalkeeper angle for the shooting angle. Now bounce the ball and move around the circle just as you did with the string in a previous drill. The goalkeeper must sense the sound of the bounce and move around her angle in the proper position to cover the shot. If you move to a spot and find that they aren't in the correct position, keep bouncing the ball until they get into the position. To add a twist, you can then kick the ball to their feet or lightly toss it to their chest for them to quickly react and catch or kick back. I like to toss it to see how quickly they react to catching it. I wouldn't do this too much but it is a good indicator to you as to whether or not they are in tune with their position.

Weak Spot for Angles

After your goalkeeper is able to move between the stroke and the end-line comfortably, you'll want to start making her move with the ball consistently. Goalkeepers always have a weak spot in their angles. I'm not sure why, but I think it may have to do with their dominate foot. If they are right-handed, the right side forty-fiveish angle (see figure 36) appears to be a weak spot. Some goalkeepers for some reason don't step far enough to their right. Now, it could have to do with the dominant foot being on that side and they are more confident or they feel their reach is farther. I don't know. But I often see balls squeak by to the right of this foot because the goalkeeper was one step off her angle in this area. So you will need to find the weak spot of your goalkeeper and really drill that side with some of these drills. You can do different variations of these drills, but the concept should be the same.

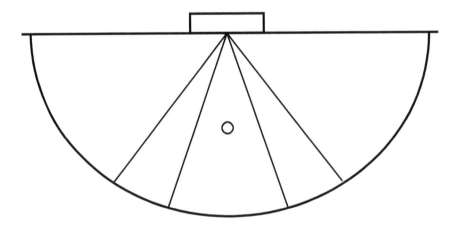

Figure 36: An example of the 45 degree angle.

Drills

I cannot emphasize enough the importance of angles, so again if you need to play the entire practice with the string set up, do it until your goalkeeper understands the concept of the imaginary lines and how angles work. The string can be used in conjunction with multiple drills. Please keep that in mind.

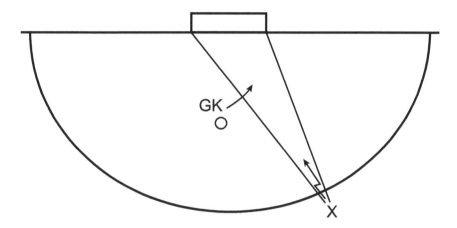

Figure 37: Take the string from previous drills and put it in the 45 degree angle area. Place a pile of balls on the 45 degree angle inside the string with a shooter. Put the goalkeeper at the stroke mark and have her move to the center of the string triangle. The shooter will then shoot to the cage and the goalkeeper must stop the ball. If she is in the correct position on the string she should have no problem stopping the ball. She will see quickly if she is correct because the string is there for a guide. Try to do this in one quick motion. You do not want her waiting for the shot; this will defeat the purpose of the drill. Do this until there is no problem with this angle. Use this idea for any problem angles. Once they understand, take away the string and do it again to see if angles have been absorbed.

chapter 4

Engaging Distance

How Far Do I Need to Be to Perform a Skill?

So many goalkeepers out there have great angles and kicks but do not know how to attack an attacker. They rush out and breakdown only to find themselves being beaten by the attacker. What a let down for the team and the goalkeeper. She did everything right. But did she?

Before we even get into advanced skills like attacking an attacker, we need to talk about the distance we need to be to do so. Now that your goalkeeper knows how to break down properly, have great angle movements, and proper kicking skills, we need to discuss engaging distance. You need to think of your goalkeeper like she is one of your defenders. You don't want your center back to go crashing into an attacker on a one versus one situation, so why would you want your goalkeeper to do that? Teach your goalkeeper the basics of defense. I actually have my goalkeepers sit in on my discussion sessions on defense and my concept of playing different scenarios out on the field. Before I teach my defenders to attack, I need to teach my defenders the distance they need to be to do so. The engaging distance is the most crucial part of the defensive techniques to learn and it requires discipline and excellent distance judgment based on each player's skill level and reach. For a defender, a jab or block tackle can only be possible if she is in the proper engaging distance. The same is true for your goalkeeper. The importance of engaging distance is to block the dangerous space to the goal and prevent the forward progress of the attacker while closing the gap between your goalkeeper and the attacker.

Engaging distance is not very easy to learn because it is fluid. If the attacker moves, the goalkeeper/defender needs to move to keep the distance pure. It requires footwork, judgment, balance, and discipline. The key is to get close enough to the attacker to be a threat to them but not too close to be eliminated. I tell my goalkeeper that this is a stick-

and-a-half-length away. No matter what, she needs to maintain that position until she can perform a skill on the attacker. This is the same for your defenders as well, although they can give more with the ball depending on the speed of the attacker.

To execute this engaging distance, your goalkeeper needs to use those breakdown steps she learned in the previous chapters and then from there quick, choppy little steps to keep her legs together while maintaining balance and moving with the attacker in the circle.

Figure 38: This is an example of stick-and-a-half-length away for engaging.

There are several ways to practice engaging distance. I like to set up grids and work in conditioning with these drills. Both will need you there to point out the engaging distance. First start with a line of cones and some sticks lined up. Have your goalkeepers run through the line and break down so that they are a stick-and-a-half-length away from the cone. This starts the concept of understanding. Then try these two drills.

Drills

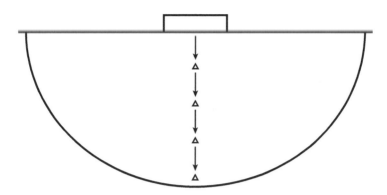

Figure 39: Have your goalkeeper start on a line. This drill does not have to be done in the circle. Place the cones 5 yards away from each other in a straight line. Have your goalkeeper pretend that the cones are the attacker and the ball. She sprints to the first cone and breaks down about 1.5 stick lengths away. Then she continues to the next cone to do the same thing. You can make this as long as you like. The important thing is for them to see where the stick-and-a-half-length is in relation to their breakdown. If you notice that they are getting too close place a different colored cone to the side of the attack cone where you want them to breakdown so that they can see the difference from where they were breaking down previously. Or you can place actual sticks to the side of the cone so that they can see where they need to breakdown. Either way, this is a good visual drill for understanding the engaging distance. You can build on this drill later in the book by adding slide tackles or stick dives on the cones after the breakdown so that they can really see the distance and why its needed.

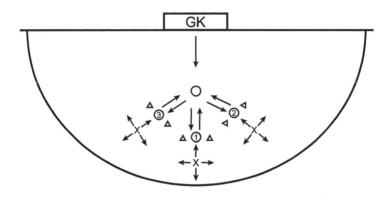

Figure 40: *You will need multiple people for this drill. Put three gates up in almost a Y shape. Place 3 people with soccer balls or basketballs behind the gates. Start with your goalkeeper just below the stroke mark at the center cone and sprint up to the stroke mark and breakdown. From here she can advance to gate 1 and breakdown at the proper engaging distance at the gate to meet her attacker. Then X and the goalkeeper should play catch for 15 seconds. X should be moving forward, backward, and side to side. The goalkeeper should be shifting and adjusting to keep the proper engaging distance from X. It is important that the goalkeeper maintains the engaging distance in the movements and makes small movements with the legs. After 15 seconds, a whistle is blown by the coach and the goalkeeper backpedals to the stroke mark. Make sure she is using her peripherals to see the stroke mark. When at the stroke mark, she sprints to the next gate and repeats the same thing. Do this for all 3 gates. End the drill with the goalkeeper backpedaling to the stroke mark and setting up square to the center of the field.*

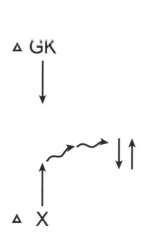

Figure 41: Have your goalkeeper start with a pool noodle in her hand. A pool noodle is just about a stick-and-a-half-length long. Have a field player, another goalkeeper, or yourself be the attacker. I often play the attacker so that they get a chance to beat up the coach. The goalkeepers all seem to enjoy it. Have each of you stand at designated areas. You as the attacker are trying to get over a line in the designated area without being hit and the goalkeeper is trying to hit you. Rules are that all hits must be below the waist. You start your run and the goalkeeper advances. She is to use the pool noodle when she is close enough to you. You tell her if it's too close. She really should be just grazing you with the tip of the noodle to be a stick-and-a-half-length away. She needs to maintain that distance from you as you move in the designated area. Try moving backwards and side to side. Make sure that the goalkeeper is staying square to you, meaning that she isn't turning her body and exposing the cage to you. Also make sure that she is using her breakdown footwork, etc. You can do this for about 10-15 seconds if she is doing a good job of moving with you. Make any variations you want with this drill; it is just a fun way to teach engaging distance.

Now is a good time to talk about footwork too. Balance is related to footwork and footwork is a basic skill of field hockey and an essential piece of goalkeeping. Effective footwork allows a goalkeeper to start and stop and change direction with quickness and balance. Footwork helps your goalkeeper prepare her body to perform a skill and it is very important for engaging distance. We already talked about the breakdown and angle movement, but with proper footwork your goalkeeper will have the ability to instantly react in any direction. Here are just a few footwork skills that are essential for engaging distance and movement in the cage.

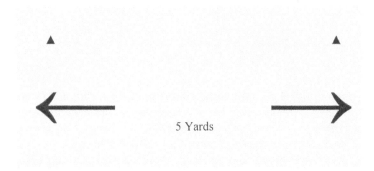

Figure 42: Start at one cone and have your goalkeeper side slide to the other cone and back. Make sure that she is keeping her body low, with her hips and shoulders facing forward. Your goalkeeper should side slide through the cones and touch them with her hand and explode to change direction.

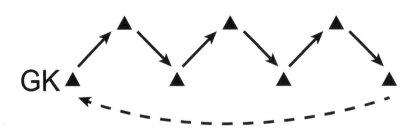

Figure 43: Start at one end, accelerate to the first cone, breakdown, drop step, and sprint to the next cone. Continue through the drill and jog back to the start. I would do this in 1-2 minute intervals, stressing staying low and on the balls of the feet, pumping arms and opening hips on the drop step and toward the cone. This works well to improve turning the hips in the angles chapter.

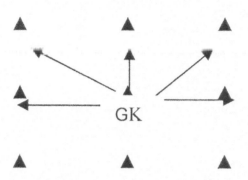

Figure 44: Begin at the center cone and sprint or side slide to each cone. Have her facing one direction so that she is working on drop stepping back to the center. This is the goalkeeper's choice. She can vary the pattern as she feels. For cones that are behind her, have her backpedal to them.

chapter 5

Advanced Skill Problems

Slide Tackling with Precision

Every goalkeeper must have the core basics down before even getting into the advanced skills. I tell my goalkeepers that although every goalkeeper looks different when she plays, the core basics are there. When you strip down the technique, you'll see that they all do the same core things in the technique, but the top part of the technique is each goalkeeper's own flare. A goalkeeper building up their repertoire of techniques should have the basics: meet the ball with the instep of the foot, all weight forward, head and hands following the ball, etc. However, each goalkeeper puts a little spin on how she executes those basic skills of kicking. It's quite a fun thing to see. I once had a goalkeeper who was a former dancer and used to pull her head over the ball quickly as if she was in a twirl. The concept was there and the ball was consistently and quickly sent out accurately. Although, she didn't fully conform to the way I played, the basic skill was there so there was no need to change the way she moved her head in the kick. That goalkeeper wound up playing at a Division I school in college. So before you go trying to fix a skill, take a hard look and make sure that the basic base of the skill is there. It may just be a tweak or, if you're lucky, nothing will need to be done with your goalkeeper's skill.

Once the base core skills are down, your goalkeeper will need to learn some advanced skills. See *Mastering the Net* for some specialty skills information. As your goalkeeper begins to learn these advanced skills, or even after they have been taught and you notice that they aren't executing them properly, you will need to fix a few things.

Slide Tackle

One advanced skill that is overused and often incorrectly is the slide tackle. I see alot of goalkeepers using this skill with their weight back. Again see *Mastering the Net* for proper positioning. This means that they are coming through the ball and they aren't seeing where it's going. You will need to work hard on getting her to tuck tighter and pull her head over and around her knees more so that she can see where the ball is moving. Start slow with no steps, just dropping into the position. Position the head where it should be every time until your goalkeeper can get into this position on her own without assistance. From there start adding a few steps to get into the skill. Keep drilling this concept in them so that it becomes a muscle-motor memory skill.

Figure 45: This is an example of a proper slide tackle.

Figure 45 (cont.): This is an example of a proper slide tackle.

Drill

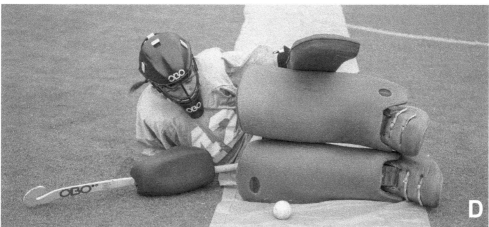

Figure 46: Use a slip and slide to help your goalkeeper work on form and technique for slide tackles and dives.

Getting Up

The next problem with slide tackles is getting up from the skill. I see all different kinds of variations here. Some goalkeeping coaches are sticklers on how to get up. I personally don't care how they get up just so long as it's quick and they are getting up facing forward with their weight going forward on the way up. You, as the coach, can decide how you want your goalkeeper to get up or let her have her own flare so long as it has the criteria that I just spoke of. If you find that your goalkeeper is leaving her weight behind, you can use this drill below to help.

Drill

Figure 47 A-D: Use a bungee cord resistance band for guiding your goalkeeper up and forward out of her slide tackle.

Legs

Another issue with the slide tackle is the legs. I see beginner goalkeepers only getting the bottom leg through the ball in time and thereby leaving a gap for the ball to be lifted over that bottom leg and under the upper leg. The goalkeeper's legs need to snap into position quickly and efficiently for the skill to be most effective. This is a hard thing to correct without them actually seeing it. Some goalkeepers just don't know that they are not pulling that top leg over fast enough. Show her how she does it, and how it should look if done properly. If you are skilled enough, thread a ball between the legs to expose the error in the skill. Now, this will take determination from your goalkeeper to really pull those legs over quickly while, in part, focusing on the head coming over and tucking tight. The only way to fix the legs is to practice. I have not really found an "outside the box" idea for this. If you have one, I'd love to hear it.

Drill

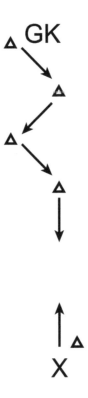

Figure 48: Place the cones in a zigzag line about 7 yards apart. Have your goalkeeper sprint to the cones and slide tackle into each one consecutively. To add more bonus to the drill, have a semi live ball at the end. The goalkeeper can get up out of the last cone and sprint to the live ball and the goalkeeper can play a true slide tackle on the ball. Another thing you can do, as your goalkeeper gets more advanced, is work on stick and glove side slide tackles as they move through the cones.

Knees

Some goalkeepers don't pull their legs over fast enough and expose their knees. All I can think is "Ouch!" By exposing the knee to the attacker, your goalkeeper runs the risk of getting hit in the knee (the one spot that doesn't have padding) by a shot.

Watch your goalkeeper closely in her slide tackle. Sometimes goalkeepers slide tackle and it doesn't look right but you can't see exactly what it is that isn't right. So, I sug-

Figure 49: This is an example of a knee being exposed during a slide tackle.

gest getting down on the ground to see her at the level that she is ending up. Ask her to slide tackle a ball or cone that is a few feet in front of you. It makes it easier to identify the problem. At this level you can see if your goalkeeper is exposing her knee first before pulling her legs into the slide tackle. There isn't much to help this issue except to start her stationary again and have her kick out her right leg into the slide tackle and drop into the slide tackle with the top leg following. Stay on the ground and have her slide tackle into where you are so you can keep watching the knee exposure and get her to pull those legs over and through faster. If you still can't see it, try videotaping and then playing it back slowly for yourself. Just by practicing the skill the proper way and with reinforcement, your goalkeeper will get better at it.

Drill

If your goalkeeper struggles to get that leg into the proper position so that she isn't showing her knee, you will want to try this drill. You will need to get yourself on the ground and on your knees. Place your hand out in front of the goalkeeper, palm facing the goalkeeper like you are saying stop, about half a foot or a foot off the ground. Have your goalkeeper about a half-stick-length away from you. Have her kick her bottom leg foot out to kick you in the hand as she is going down into her slide tackle. Obviously this is done at half speed so that you don't get run over by your goalkeeper. Do this numerous times until the knee is no longer exposed in the kick and the legs are tucking quickly.

Timing

Another issue with slide tackles is the timing. This one can be a doozy for some goalkeepers. Some goalkeepers will use the skill too late or too early and get burned by the attacker. I have several things that I do to try to get the concept of engaging distance across to goalkeepers. See also chapter 4, Engaging Distance.

Drill

Another drill to try to work this problem is figures 39 and 48. This drill will work not only engaging distance but also timing.

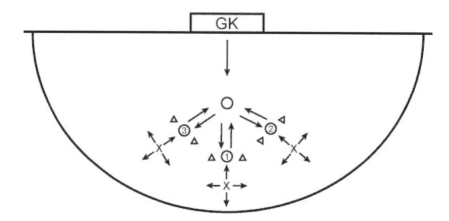

Figure 50: In this drill, put three gates up in almost a Y shape. Place 3 people at the gates. Give your goalkeeper a noodle. Have your goalkeeper start at the center cone and sprint up to the stroke mark. At the stroke mark, have your goalkeeper sprint to gate 1 and then breakdown at the proper engaging distance at the gates. Then X should be moving forward, backward, and side to side. The goalkeeper should be shifting and adjusting to keep the proper engaging distance from X. She needs to try to move so fast to hit X in the legs with the tip of her noodle. If she catches X in the middle of the noodle, she's too close and should retreat back to the proper engaging distance. If she misses, that's OK. She should only miss by a few inches though to keep the proper engaging distance. After 10 seconds, a whistle is blown by the coach and the goalkeeper backpedals to the stroke mark. Make sure she is using her peripherals to see the stroke mark. When at the stroke mark, she sprints to the next gate and repeats the same thing. Do this for all 3 gates. End the drill with the goalkeeper backpedaling to the stroke mark and setting up square to the center of the field.

Alignment

One last error that I see in slide tackles is the alignment on the slide tackle. This is why some goalkeepers get burned by the attacker. You will hear the concept "line your belly button with the ball" or "line your core up with the ball" from some goalkeeping coaches. This is true, but goalkeepers first need to understand what that means. Just like you had to do earlier, you will need to have your goalkeeper just drop into the slide tackle from her basic stance and reposition her into the tuck. Place the ball in front of her just below the knees and out far enough that if she takes a peek with her head, she can see the ball. Now have her stand again. Have her drop back into the tuck. The ball should not move and should be aligned with the exact spot you placed it in, just below the knees and far enough out that she can see it if she peeks with her head around her knees. Keep doing this drill so that the concept of the belly button lined up with the ball sinks in a little for your goalkeeper.

Figure 51: An example of a goalkeeper peeking at the ball in a slide tackle position. Have your goalkeeper get into her slide tackle position. Place a ball just in front of the legs at the knee area. Have her tuck her head forward. She should easily see the ball if her head is in the proper position. Emphasize this position and the importance of being able to find the ball when she is down on the ground.

Drill

If you find that your goalkeeper is not dropping into the correct position, I suggest chalking out the spot.

Have your goalkeeper lie down in the proper slide tackle position. Move her into the position and make adjustments. Then use baby powder and chalk out the position. Have your goalkeeper then get up into her basic stance. Now have her drop into a slide tackle without sliding. She can use the chalk positioning as a guide for proper positioning. Have her do this multiple times until you think she understands it. Another suggestion would be to put a string in a straight line from the ball to behind your goalkeeper.

You will need to get your goalkeeper moving once she has mastered the stationary position. Start slow with two to three steps, then build up speed to get into the skill as your goalkeeper gets more confident with the new core technique.

Figure 52: Use the string from earlier drills and attach it to the center of the cage and pull it straight out to the top of the circle. Place a ball on the line anywhere between the stroke and the top of the circle. Have your goalkeeper stand bisecting the line in her basic stance and a comfortable position behind the stroke mark. Have her sprint up and slide tackle the ball keeping her run straight with the string. In addition, have her pull her knees on the slide tackle and through the slide. Her knees should tuck and line up with the string on the slide tackle.

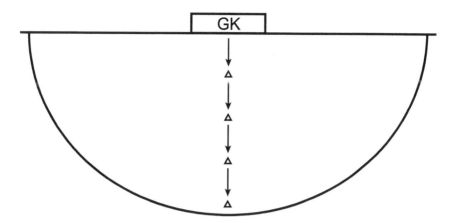

Figure 53: Place 4 cones in a straight line about 10 yards apart. Place a ball on top of each cone. Have your goalkeeper start about 5 yards behind the bottom cone. Have your goalkeeper sprint to the first cone and slide tackle it. Have her get up quickly and sprint to the next cone to slide tackle it. Continue the drill through all the cones.

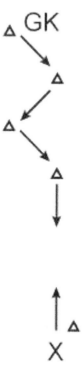

Figure 54: Place four cones on the field about 10 yards apart. Place them in a zigzag line. Have your goalkeeper start about 5 yards behind the bottom cone. Have your goalkeeper sprint to the first cone and slide tackle it. Have her get up quickly and change direction and sprint to the next cone to slide tackle it. Continue the drill through all the cones.

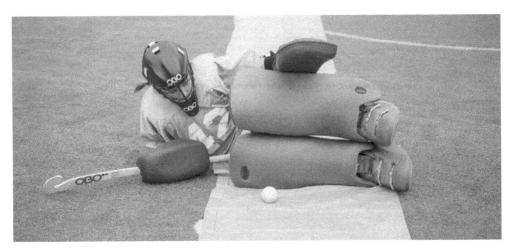

Figure 55: Once again, pull out the slip and slide; place a ball just inside the beginning of the slide. Have your goalkeeper advance to the ball and slide tackle the ball on the slip and slide.

Advanced Slide Tackling: Attacking the Other Side

Although I don't see anyone teaching slide tackling to the glove side anymore, nor do I see it used outside of my team, I still think it's an essential piece that goalkeepers should have in their repertoire.

I teach my goalkeeper to use both sides of the slide tackle, but only after she has perfected the stick side. The reason I want my goalkeeper to be able to slide tackle to both sides of her body is because I have my goalkeeper play aggressively on the endline. It will depend on your coaching philosophy if you want to teach your goalkeeper to be able to tackle on the glove side of her body. The slide tackle to the glove side covers all the same concepts as the stick side, except it's the other side of the body. The stick is where the glove would be – just above the top leg and ready for an aerial. The head is over the top, thereby pulling all the weight forward. The legs are scrunched up and aimed belly button to the ball. She slides into this the same way she does for the stick side. For most goalkeepers, it's extremely awkward until it's a muscle-motor memory skill. Emphasize everything we talked about for the stick-side slide tackle with her head over to peek at the ball, tight tuck, aim her belly button to ball, etc.

Figure 56: An example of a glove-side slide tackle.

Drill

You can repurpose some earlier drills to work on this side. Use figures 48, 52, 53 and 54 to help with this skill. Do keep in mind that this is an advanced skill and should only be used when your goalkeeper has perfected the stick-side slide tackle.

When Is This Used?

I think goalkeepers are not taught this anymore because we haven't fully defined when to use this skill. I have my goalkeeper use it for one purpose: when our defenders are getting beat on the right side of the circle at the endline. I want my goalkeeper to be able to step off of her angle a little to prevent a pass to the stroke off the endline so I have my goalkeeper play aggressively here. This is my coaching philosophy in this area. I usually tell her just about at what spot to advance and how I want her to step off. We work on this throughout the year with attackers coming in at different paces and in different ways. You will need to find your own coaching philosophy here. Anyway, my goalkeeper uses the glove-side slide tackle on the right endline as a double-team situation. I like this because her legs, the tallest part of her, are now keeping the ball from going along the endline and she is now in a position to play a pass with her glove or she can roll and reach with her stick. In addition, she now keeps the ball in front and is in a better position to see the ball deflection to get up and play. Not to mention, the ability to recoil from here to play the ball.

Figure 57: An example of a goalkeeper slide tackling on her glove side being attacked by an endline attacker.

My Goalkeeper's Been Beat – Now What?

Well, you thought your goalkeeper had the attacker on the one-versus-one situation, but something happened. The technique was off or the timing went bad. So now what should your goalkeeper do? First thing, she should stretch. Depending on what end of your goalkeeper the attacker chooses to go around is where your goalkeeper should stretch. For instance, if the attacker chooses to pull around the goalkeeper's feet, the goalkeeper should push and stretch her legs out and point her toes. With any luck, the attacker will have pulled the ball short, and the goalkeeper can help slow her down by creating a larger obstacle for her. The same goes for the head side of the goalkeeper, although the goalkeeper will have more control to this side. The goalkeeper's stick is a handy tool in these situations. Have your goalkeeper lock her wrist to make it firm and try to hold the ball from passing. If your goalkeeper can manage to slow the attacker down for a second, she will give your defense a chance to get back and help her.

Figure 58:An example of a goalkeeper pointing her toes and stretching into position to save the ball.

Figure 59: An example of a goalkeeper stretching her upper body to try to trap the ball.

The next thing to do is to get up and get back on her angle. This is why getting up quickly and accurately from these down positions is crucial. Have your goalkeeper get up from this down position and sprint on her angle to the goal. She should be prepared for a quick shot. Once an attacker sees an open cage, she will release quickly after she beats your goalkeeper. I tell my goalkeepers that this movement is a desperation movement. If she is quick at getting up and the attacker isn't quick, she has a shot at saving the ball. The important thing here is to emphasize to her that it is possible for the ball to be saved. I've seen it happen. Do not let her give up and watch the attacker put the ball in the cage. Every effort needs to be made to keep the ball out of the cage here. Too many times I've seen an attacker miss the cage because she got excited about the open cage. Your goalkeeper should want the glory for helping keep that ball out.

Drills

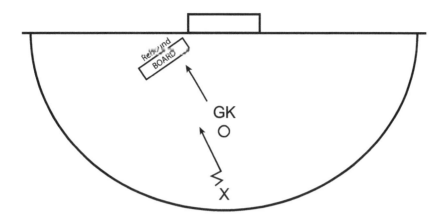

Figure 60: Have your goalkeeper start in her normal position at the stroke mark. Place rebound boards on either side of her outside the posts and on an angle so that when the ball hits it, the ball will ricochet in the cage. Start first with your goalkeeper on her feet. Hit balls to the rebound boards and have your goalkeeper sprint on her feet back to save the ball. Work both sides of the cage. Then have your goalkeeper dive back to save the ball. Work both sides of the cage. Then advance this drill by adding a shot directly to the goalkeeper for a kick then a shot to the boards for a dive back to save the ball.

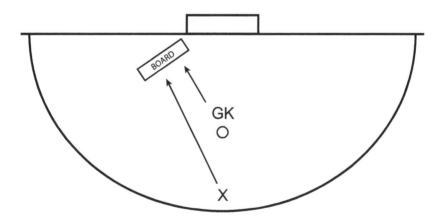

Figure 61: Have your goalkeeper start in her normal position at the stroke mark but down in a slide tackle or stick dive position. Place rebound boards on either side of her outside the posts and on an angle so that when the ball hits it, the ball will ricochet in the cage. Say "Go" and count to "One-Mississippi" before hitting the ball to the rebound boards. Your goalkeeper should get up on "Go" and dive backwards for the save. Work both sides of the cage. To advance this drill, add a live element and have your goalkeeper slide tackle or stick dive a real player. Have that player then retrieve the ball and send it to the board so that your goalkeeper has to get up and dive back to save the ball. Work both sides.

My Goalkeeper Falls to Her Knees

I see younger players who have not had any formal training fall to their knees instead of slide tackling. You'll find a goalkeeper who hasn't had formal training and is working off of instincts will drop to her knees to play a ball. Also, I sometimes see this happen to intermediate goalkeepers who haven't been taught to slide tackle. She has the aggressive nature and wants to advance but doesn't know how, or she panics, in her decision-making and drops to her knees to make a play. The good news is that she has the aggressive nature to advance to the play and her timing is usually correct. The bad news is she isn't performing a skill. As long as I've been working, I haven't found any solid "out the box" idea to fix this mistake. What I have found, is if you give her the information on all the skills and help her with her decision-making for those skills, the dropping to her knees disappears. But in the meantime, try to emphasize to her that there is only one spot on her body that has no padding and no coverage whatsoever and that's her knees. If she bends or goes down on her knees she is fully exposing this area to the attacker. By doing so, her knees are now vulnerable to a straight shot and without any padding, this can be dangerous for her. Once you explain that, she will try to focus on not doing it. If you see it happen again, you take away your goalkeeper's security blanket – the stick. You can also replace the stick with a pool noodle. Depending on the goalkeeper, I usually take the stick away for the rest of practice. I find that once I take away the stick in my young goalkeeper, they don't play as confident and thereby do not attack with their knees. This will condition your goalkeeper to think before she acts next time because she doesn't want to lose her stick again.

Figure 62: An example of a goalkeeper playing with a pool noodle.

chapter 6

Recoil or Worm

What's That?

The recoil is more of an instinctual skill for most goalkeepers. It's mostly a scramble or last-ditch effort to get the ball when your goalkeeper is down. Nonetheless, I work with my goalkeeper to strengthen the skills for this so that it can be done effectively and she will be more successful in the goal. The recoil is called such because the goalkeeper is springing herself in the air and inching herself to try to intercept a lifted shot when she is down on the ground.

Figure 63: An example of a recoil.

Technique

Start with your goalkeeper on the ground on her stick side, as if she has done a stick dive or slide tackle. It can be taught for both sides of the body, but first start with the dominant side (stick side). Have her tuck everything in tight, while still on her side. Have her push off with her wrist and elbow of her stick hand, her right hip, and her right ankle. My goalkeeper also uses her glove hand to help with this propel as well. She pushes hard and up, exploding into the air. Your goalkeeper should reach for the ball with her hands. Her legs should just drop behind. If done right, your goalkeeper should get a decent amount of air between her and the turf as well as have moved herself about one foot from the original position. Please have your goalkeeper try this without a ball, but have her eyes focused on something in the leap so that she isn't looking down. Keep in mind that there is no nice way to land for this skill and it can be rough on the body. Practicing this skill should be short and if possible, use a mat to soften the blow to the body and preserve your goalkeeper for game time.

Figure 64: A recoil broken down.

Drills

Start with your goalkeeper lying down in a stick dive across the cage. Send tosses to her about 24 inches in the air above her stick. The height will depend on your goalkeeper. Stretch the limit for your goalkeeper to see how high she can push herself into the air. Work all different heights and work both sides of the goalkeeper.

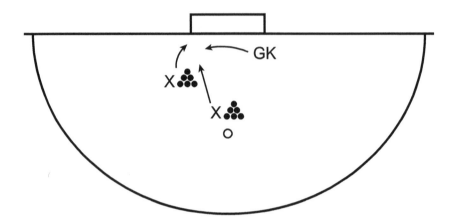

Figure 65: You will need at least two people for this drill. Start with your goalkeeper on a post. Have her drop step and do a stick dive across the goalmouth to save a ball coming to the opposite corner. Then have the second person send a toss to the goalkeeper so that she has to recoil to save it. Advance this drill by adding a second toss. Work all different heights and work both sides of the goalkeeper.

chapter 7

Advanced Skill Problems

Diving with Confidence

I find it interesting that there are alot of goalkeepers out there who are aggressive and will kick with precision and slide tackle well but when asked to dive, shy away from it. Our society has taught our goalkeepers that being aggressive is good but getting dirty isn't. We need to change this thought. Alot of field hockey goalkeeper issues have to do with her confidence in the dive. Goalkeepers are concerned they will get beat, or do it wrong, and hurt themselves. Whatever the reason, we need to fix this mentality. I'm not saying that goalkeepers should be on the ground all the time, but I do think that there are times that warrant a dive. Plus, it will help if your goalkeeper has the skill in her repertoire to choose when defending the goal. To learn how to properly dive to different sides, check out *Mastering the Net*.

Figure 66: The goalkeeper dives to save the ball. She extends her stick and arm with palms facing the ball. She contacts the ground on her side with her eyes focused on the ball.

Stick Dives

Stick dives are for balls that are out of reach of the goalkeeper's feet. There are two types of stick dives: stick dives for aerials and stick dives for balls on the ground. The stick becomes an extension of the arm for blocking and saving balls. From her basic stance, the goalkeeper then takes a step with the foot nearest the ball and leaps into a dive to save the ball. This leap can be a slide along the ground or a leap into the air (see figure 63). Like with all other skills, the goalkeeper should always position her head and chest behind the ball. It is crucial that the head remain as close as possible to the line of the ball. I see diving done very often with a goalkeeper landing on her belly. Not only is that bad for her chest, but it will inevitably knock the wind out of her. The other thing to point out is that the height that the goalkeeper covers is smaller when she lands on her belly. Have your goalkeeper lie on her side and measure the height from the ground to the top of her side. Now have your goalkeeper lie on her belly and measure the height from the ground to the top of her back. By turning on to her stomach, she covers less surface area and less of the cage. This goes for when she is in the air or on the ground. So not only for her safety, but also to cover more area of the cage, you will want her to stay on her side.

I have found a few "outside the box" ideas to help correct this bad habit.

Figure 67: Here is an example of how you can show your goalkeeper the benefits of landing on your side. Have your goalkeeper lie on her belly, face down on the ground. Measure from the ground to the top of her back and show her the measurement. Now move her to her side, facing out and measure from the ground to the top of her side. Show her that measurement and make the comparison. Which one will she be most successful at stopping the ball just by surface area alone?

Drills

Whenever you are first teaching a skill like this that may intimidate your goalkeeper, it is important you start in a safety crouch to give them a sense of comfort. Have your goalkeeper start in a low safety crouch with her rear-end hitting her heels. Then have her lean to her stick side and slide her stick along the ground until she is flat on the ground on her side. Her legs should just follow. Practice this several times so that she gets the hang of it and understands how to properly dive. Every time she lands on the ground, adjust her positioning as needed to try to train her body the muscle-motor memory of where she needs to be when she lands. From here you can slowly work your way into a half-way between the safety crouch and basic stance start. Have her dive from this position a few times until she understands it. If you feel confident that she can move into diving from a basic stance, then do some dives from this position as well.

I use two guides for my goalkeeper when she is first learning to dive. I just teach her to go and it's usually out to her right or left. Stand her on the end-line and have her dive along this line focusing on the line and keeping her body parallel with the line. As she gets more advanced you will want to teach her that she needs to attack a player on the front 45 of her body (explained later on). Use the lacrosse lines on your field and have your goalkeeper dive along these lines to understand the front 45 of her body dive.

Timing

An essential piece to stick dives is timing and engaging distance. See the chapter on engaging distance for more information. If your goalkeeper gets too close to an attacker before performing a skill she will be late in trying to retrieve the ball and essentially behind the play. If she's too far away from the attacker when she performs the skill, then the attacker has plenty of time to maneuver around your goalkeeper and get to the goal. So engaging distance and timing will help your goalkeeper with performing many skills. It is important that you have her practice the engaging distance drills from Chapter 4. If she doesn't understand them then you cannot move on to higher-level skills until she does.

Now, let's first talk about stick dives that are on the ground and intentional to cut off an attacker or intercept a ball. Have your goalkeeper practice stick dives for when there is a one-versus-one situation on the field. I tell my goalkeeper to cut off her attacker on the front 45 of her body.

Front 45, Flat, Back 45 Angle Stick Dives

I try to tell my goalkeepers, just like I would my field players to think of themselves as a clock. The body is the center of the clock. Directly in front of her is 12 o'clock and directly behind her is 6 o'clock. With that in mind, directly to her right side is 3 o'clock and directly to her left side is 9 o'clock. So now that we have established the clock in relation to her body, I tell my goalkeeper that when attacking an offender in a stick dive, she needs to attack on the front 45 angle of her body. That is at the 10 or 11 and 1 or 2 o'clock positions of her body (see figure 68). I want her to attack in the front positions not only to keep the ball in front of her but also to give herself a second or possibly third attempt if she misses. There are two more positions that she can attack. 1.) The flat angle (the 3 and 9 position) or 2). The back 45 angle (4 or 5 and the 7 or 8 position). If for some reason your goalkeeper gets beat on her front 45 angle, she then has, let's hope, the flat angle, and then the back 45 angle to try to save the ball again from going in the cage. If anything, she at least has the back 45 angle (which I often tell my goalkeeper is a desperation dive) to try to save the ball. This is often a scramble and will look sloppy, but that extra time helps your goalkeeper to be more successful with stopping the ball. If you start your goalkeeper with doing dives on the flat angle to attack an offender, she will only have the back 45 angle, if that, to try to save the ball.

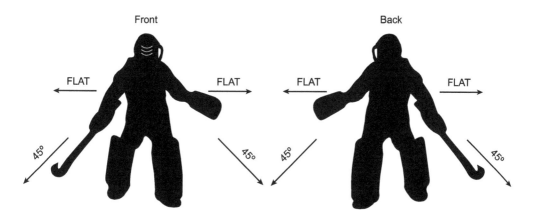

Figure 68: This is where the front 45, back 45 and even or flat positions are in relation to the goalkeeper and her attacker.

Drill

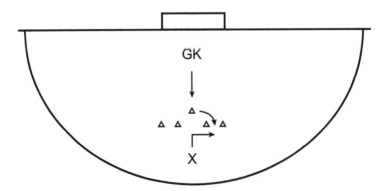

Figure 69: Set up two gates like a Y shape. Start with an attacker on the top of the Y and the goalkeeper in her normal position in the circle. Have your goalkeeper advance to an attacker. The attacker is to advance to the goalkeeper and pull right just in front of the gates. The goalkeeper must then stick dive through the gates to cut off the attacker's pulls to the right. Work both sides.

A stick dive can be used for intercepting a pass too. I mainly have my goalkeeper do the front 45 dives when she is coming off the post to intercept a pass. You want your goalkeeper to keep the ball to one side of the field, so by intercepting a pass across the goalmouth she is keeping her defense in the proper position to play the ball successfully to keep it out of the goal. By diving on the front 45 on a ball being passed off the endline back toward the stroke, your goalkeeper is again cutting off the ball before it gets behind her and keeping the ball in a better position for her angles. She keeps the ball in a Zone 2 or 3 so that it makes it more difficult for an attacker to score.

Drill

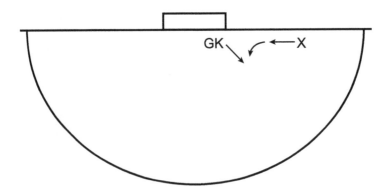

Figure 70: Have your goalkeeper stand on the post of the cage. Have an attacker on the endline who will be sending a pass to the stroke mark. Have your goalkeeper read the pass and cut the ball off on the front 45. Work both sides of the cage.

Staying Strong

Sometimes a stick dive is used as a last effort in a scramble and your goalkeeper is out of position or knows she is going to get beaten. The goalkeeper must scramble to clear the ball out of the danger zone. Often times in this type of dive, the goalkeeper has no power as to where the ball will be redirected. That's why focus and following the ball's movement is important. Your goalkeeper should try to keep the ball in front of her for protection, but being on the ground after the dive creates vulnerability. The only thing a goalkeeper can do in this situation is be a strong wall. She must lie there with arms and legs extended in front of her, prepared for a flick and ready to react. She can trap the ball with her stick and try to hold it in front of her. She should keep her wrist firm and angle the stick to block. You will want to work this situation and strengthen your goalkeeper's stick wrist. In addition, this can be used in conjunction with the recoil (see chapter 6). When working with your goalkeeper on this, work multiple scenarios working both sides of the body.

Figure 71: Pull the slip and slide back out and have your goalkeeper on one end of it. Roll a ball and have her slide along the mat to retrieve the ball. This is a fun way to get them diving and it works great for hot days too. Make sure you work both sides (regular and reverse stick dives).

Drills

Figure 72: Have your goalkeeper lie out like she would if she were in a stick dive position. Now have a pile of balls about 3-4 feet away. Hit each ball at her stick. Have her hold strong to stop the ball. This requires a very strong wrist. This will also work for upper-level goalkeepers that lie down for corners. You can move closer or farther away. As a bonus to this drill, place a ramp just in front of the stick, so that when you hit the ramp, the ball is lifted in to the air. This will train your goalkeeper to watch the ball all the way in to her stick and get used to lifting it or using the glove to stop those. This is great to work on tipped balls while the goalkeeper is down on the ground.

Figure 73: You need to do this drill with your defensive players. Have your defensive players facing you in the circle with their backs to the goalkeeper. Start with your goalkeeper on the ground in a stick dive position. Take a pile of balls and hit them to her stick. With a firm hand and with her glove she should be stopping the ball in front of her body. Have your goalkeeper say "Help." The defensive players should turn and the one closest should call for the ball and come to the goalkeeper's aid to control the ball off of the goalkeeper and escort the ball out of danger. As the ball is being removed, work your goalkeeper with getting up with the ball and staying behind the ball as it is being escorted out of the danger zone. Once the ball is being removed out of the danger, the goalkeeper should be getting up and in her basic stance. All defensive players should be moving in support with the ball.

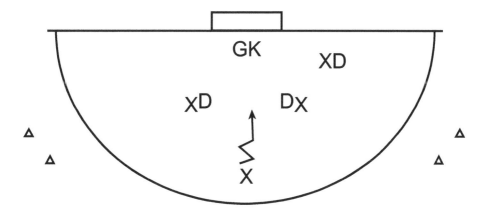

Figure 74: You need to do this drill with your defensive players and one attacker. Have your defensive players facing you in the circle with their backs to the goalkeeper. Start with your goalkeeper on the ground in a stick dive position. Take a pile of balls and hit them to her stick. With a firm hand and with her glove she should be stopping the ball in front of her body. Have your goalkeeper say "Help." The defensive players should turn and the one closest should call for the ball and come to the goalkeeper's aid. The attacker should reach in and pull the ball back and scoop it over the goalkeeper. This is where the goalkeeper needs to recoil to make the save. Then the defender is to come in and control the ball off of the goalkeeper and escort the ball out of danger. Once the ball is being removed out of the danger, the goalkeeper should be getting up and in her basic stance. All defensive players should be moving in support with the ball. Give the defenders a gate to work the ball towards. Advance this drill by asking your goalkeeper to get up and clear the ball after the recoil, then have the defensive players react to the ball afterwards.

Figure 75: Start with your goalkeeper on the ground in a stick dive position. Place a ramp just in front of the stick and another in front of the legs. Take a pile of balls and hit them to the ramp at her stick. With a firm wrist and with her glove she should be stopping the ball in front of her body. Work this area for a while to strengthen the wrist and reaction time on tips. Do the same for the ramp at the legs. Have your goalkeeper lift the top leg up like she is scissoring her legs. She needs to do this to save the ball. Work this area until the reaction timing is there.

Aerial Dives

There are all kinds of aerial dives. There are aerial dives for strokes (which are the most common). There are aerial dives for corner style lifts that might catch the goalkeeper off guard, or aerials for balls out of reach in normal field of play. Aerial dives for strokes we will get to later in Chapter 11. The concept for aerial dives during corners and in normal play is the same. Always go with hands, get a good leap and follow the ball all the way in to the hands. The legs and the rest of the body just follow along. Again, we want to make sure that your goalkeeper is landing on her side for these dives. *Mastering the Net* will give you the basics for diving, but the most important thing I can stress for you to reiterate to your goalkeeper is following the ball all the way in to the hands and just to take a leap of faith. For aerial dives, you need to get your goalkeeper comfortable with landing and understanding how far she can leap. Not just height distance but length distance. Every goalkeeper you will teach will have a different height and length distance that they can reach and you will need to be aware of it as well. If I didn't know that about my goalkeeper I wouldn't be able to say — "You can get that" or "That was too far for you to reach, next time do this." It's a fine balance between demanding they reach it and knowing if physically they can. These types of dives are hard on the body and hard to simulate. But we as coaches can always try.

Figure 76: An example of an aerial dive.

Drill

Start with your goalkeeper in a safety crouch and have her fall while catching a tossed ball at her. These should be easy falls, but it helps your goalkeeper to get used to falling.

Another idea is to talk to your track coach and see if you can borrow a few mats. Place a mat on either side of the cage. Have your goalkeeper stand in the middle a little out toward the attacker. Now send tosses to the posts of the cage. Have your goalkeeper dive to catch them or move her body fast enough to get to the post to catch the ball. The mats are there to help the wear and tear on the body for the dives. I find this works well with footballs. Have your goalkeeper catch and tuck the ball in to her. This will be a useful drill for strokes as well.

Getting Up

Sometimes when a goalkeeper is on the ground in these situations, she will go to her back and then push herself up. This needs to be fixed so that your goalkeeper is getting up with her weight forward and her eye on the ball like she does with all the other skills. Again, I don't really care how she gets up just so long as the criteria are met. If you find that her weight is back use the same concept from figure 47 in the slide tackle chapter. I always work some type of drill with my goalkeeper on the ground and getting up, not only to strengthen her but also to try to speed her up when she pushes off the ground. If you work some of these concepts in your goalkeeping warm-up you'll see a difference in speed coming off the ground.

Drills

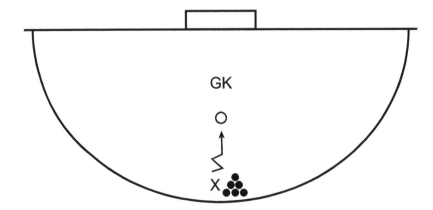

Figure 77: Place all the balls at the top of the circle. Start with your goalkeeper on her belly. The hitter should say "Up!" and the goalkeeper pushes off the ground and into her basic stance. Have her then run in place until the ball is hit. The hitter should count, in her head, to 3 slowly before hitting the ball to the goalkeeper. Once the goalkeeper makes the clear, she should get down into a push up again. This should be a continuous drill. Start with 6 continuous balls and work your way up to 10. Advance this drill by adding targets for the clears.

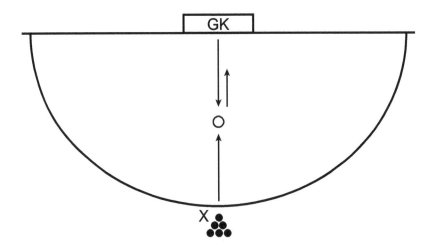

Figure 78: Place all the balls at the top of the circle. Start with your goalkeeper on goalmouth in her basic stance. The hitter should say "Go!" and the goalkeeper sprints to the stroke mark and backpedals. On the backpedal send a ball to the goalkeeper. After the clear, she is to sprint back up to the stroke mark and backpedal again. This should be a continuous drill. Start with 6 continuous balls and work your way up to 10. Advance this drill by adding targets for the clears. You can also have your goalkeeper do a push up between the balls and before the sprint up to the stroke mark. Add on to this drill by having your goalkeeper start on her belly in the goalmouth and getting up to sprint on the "Go."

When to Use

There are different scenarios that call for dives. Unfortunately, the game of field hockey is an evolving game and nothing is in black and white so knowing when to use a skill will come with experience. However, there are some situations that I try to have my goalkeeper look out for. Once she uses the skill a few times for these situations, it sticks in her mind and she will begin to understand when to use it and when not to. Of course, you will need to guide your goalkeeper through this, but this hopefully will give you a starting guide to use.

Now, we can't have our goalkeepers just going out and attacking field players that are trying to score. There are 10 other people on the field who she needs to work with. So she should use the stick dives for shootouts (1 vs. goalkeeper) or breakaways towards the circle. Another time would be if the ball changed direction across the goalmouth. She can stick dive across the goalmouth to save the ball. Another time, you can tell your goalkeeper to use it is for when the attacker is dribbling the endline and looking to pass. A stick dive to intercept that pass is a great option to choose. You will need to work this with your goalkeeper so that she knows the distance that she can make with a stick dive and she can work on timing the ball. Again, with some practice and some experience, she can do this with confidence.

Drill

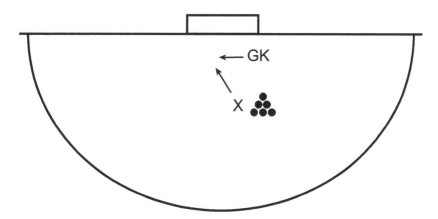

Figure 79: This is a broken phase of end-line balls. But it should be practiced alot. Have your goalkeeper standing on the post and facing the sideline. Have a pile of balls at the stroke mark. X says "Turn" and counts "1 Mississippi" and sends the ball to the far post. The goalkeeper drop steps, with the inside foot, along the goalmouth and dives across the goalmouth to save the ball. Work different distances to keep your goalkeeper honest. A bonus to this drill is to add a second ball that is a lift from the saved ball.

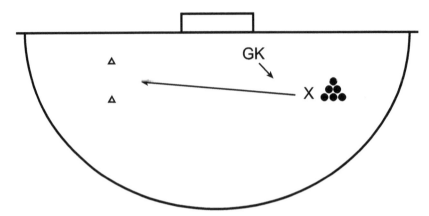

Figure 80: Have your goalkeeper standing on the post and facing the side-line. Have a pile of balls at the stroke mark. Place X about 2-3 yards off of the end-line and have her send quick hard passes across the circle to a specific target. The goalkeeper needs to dive to intercept the hard pass.

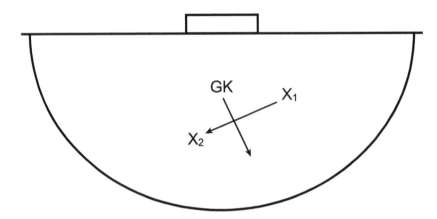

Figure 81: You will need other people for this drill. Have 2 attackers inside the circle and have them about 7-10 yards apart. Have your goalkeeper behind the stroke mark and the attackers in front of the goalkeeper on an angle and about 5 yards from the goalkeeper. Have X1 pass to X2 and have your goalkeeper try to intercept the pass. Have these passes increase speed as the goalkeeper gets better at intercepting them. Do this all over the circle in different areas.

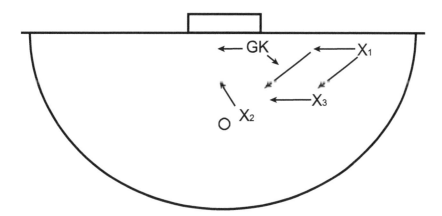

Figure 82: Let's put all that we worked on together in one drill. You will need 3 attackers for this drill. Have X1 dictate where she wants to send the ball. X1 can dribble to the goalkeeper and then pass to X2. X2 will receive and send to the far post. X1 can also send to X3 who can send across the goalmouth to X2 on the opposite side of the goal. If you want to add more challenge you can have X1 also dribble to the goalkeeper and try to go through her.

Like I said, there are many other times that your goalkeeper can use a stick dive, but these are just a few that you can drill and work on with your goalkeeper so that she can get confident with when and how to use the skill. Once she begins to use it for these scenarios, she will begin to see other times that it can be used.

Glove and Stick Aerial Saves

Now that we have covered stick dives on the ground, we need to discuss stick and glove dives in the air. I find these mainly to be instinctual in goalkeepers, but it can be practiced. This skill is a dive in the air to stop a ball. I find that when a goalkeeper does this instinctually, she is reaching for the ball with her stick. What you want to tell your goalkeeper is to aim to catch the ball with her chest behind the ball. For better understanding, watch a football player catch a ball. Most of the time, he catches at chest level and brings the ball in to his body. You want to teach your goalkeeper to do the same concept. Tell your goalkeeper to think of stopping the ball with her chest for several reasons. 1. The chest covers more surface area. 2. Your goalkeeper will push off harder and not reach toward the ball. 3. It helps your goalkeeper to land on her side. 4. I mentioned that the hands have weight and purpose; everything comes out of the core of the body. You don't want your goalkeeper to reach for the ball because then she has nowhere to extend later. Of course, there are times where reaching comes into play, but you want your goalkeeper to try to make contact with the ball from the core of the body and push out.

Figure 83: An example of an aerial dive.

My issue with practicing this skill is that the body can only take so much repeated diving. You may need to do these dives into a sand pit, onto a large gymnastics or high jump-type mat, or even into a pool.

Drill

Talk to your track coach and see if you can use the high jump mat or the sand pit. Use a soccer ball or football and have your goalkeeper in her basic stance. You can chose to do this with or without equipment on your goalkeeper. Send tosses to the mat or sand pit and have your goalkeeper jump into the air landing on the mat or sand pit and catching the ball. Work both sides of your goalkeeper. Do this drill until your goalkeeper is comfortable with diving and reaching with her chest behind the ball. Make sure that your goalkeeper is trying to catch the ball with her chest behind the ball. This will help when you start using a field hockey ball and with large bounds towards the ball.

Figure 84: Use your bungee resistance cord for this drill. Have your goalkeeper in her basic stance. A coach will be on the other end of the bungee giving your goalkeeper resistance. A player will be at the stroke mark and will be sending flicks to one side of the cage. Focus on one side at a time. Have your goalkeeper extend and reach for this toss, trying to come in contact with the ball with her chest. Remember to always go with hands to the ball. The coach will add some resistance to the aerial extension that your goalkeeper is trying to perform and slowly give and release with the goalkeeper so that your goalkeeper can land properly. I actually just walk forward with the goalkeeper so that she can perform the skill but I'm adding resistance to her the entire time she is trying to come in contact with the ball. Do this several times and then take the bungee off and let your goalkeeper perform the skill on her own without resistance. Notice the distance your goalkeeper now gets with her extension to the ball. You should use resistance training once a week so that your goalkeeper gets stronger and is more capable of extending farther out to come in contact with the ball.

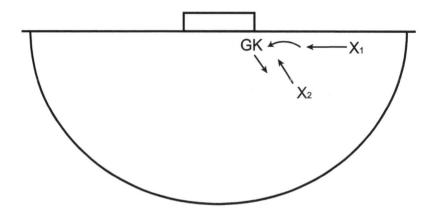

Figure 85: Have your goalkeeper start on the post and X1 just past the corner hash on the end-line. X2 will be positioned at the 5 yard hash and 3-5 yards off the end-line. X1 will dribble toward the goalkeeper and engage the goalkeeper. She can lift or try to shoot or even come in far enough that the goalkeeper has to slide tackle. You can vary it on your own. Once X1 is done have X2 either retrieve the rebound and lift or shoot or take from a pile of balls and lift or shoot. This is a great way to work recoils if it's done fast and when the goalkeeper is down.

Defense: What Can Your Defense Do to Help a Goalkeeper When She Is Down?

Here is the crucial part that you need to work with your defense and goalkeeper. Your goalkeeper has now done her job and made an impeccable save by either attacking with a stick dive or saving an aerial shot. When these types of saves happen, you'll see your defense watch the ball and stare in awe of the play. Which in a way, you can't blame them. It probably was a sight to see, but the game is still going and your goalkeeper still needs your defense's help. This is where you need to teach your defense what to do in these situations. Through my years of coaching, every coach feels differently about how to handle these. Some coaches will assign one person only to handle any loose balls coming off the goalkeeper. Other coaches just teach their entire defensive unit how to handle these loose balls so that the closest personnel can take care of it. I'm a fan of "knowledge is power," and if you teach the entire unit to do it, there will be no worries when the time comes for it to happen. First, tell your defense that if your goalkeeper is down on the ground, they need to tightly defend. Second, they need to be aware that if the ball is out in front of the goalkeeper, they need to help "escort" the ball outside of the circle. I try to teach my defenders to come through with their backs to the center of the field to protect the ball from the attackers and to dribble the ball out of danger. Passing right away can create another scurry in the circle. Positive possession is best.

Drill

Figure 86: This is how a defender should take the ball off the goalkeeper.

Practicing this is very easy. I suggest you take some time out of every week, at least in the first few weeks of the season to practice this skill. You want your defense to react right away when something like this happens.

Drill

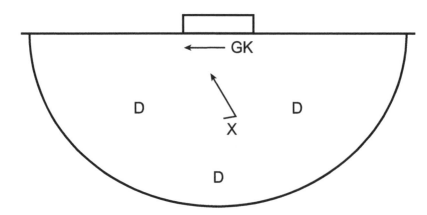

Figure 87: Now that we have learned how to take the ball off the goalkeeper, let's work on when it should be done and quick reactions to it. Start with X at the stroke and goalkeeper on the post facing the sideline. Position 3 defenders around the circle with their backs to the cage. Blow the whistle and have your goalkeeper drop step as if the ball has been passed from the end-line and up to the stroke. Have X send the ball to the far post and the goalkeeper should be diving to save the ball. Have her calling for the ball and when she is down on the ground saying "help." At that moment, the defenders are to turn and collect the ball from the goalkeeper. If you choose for one player to collect the ball, have the others keep their backs to the ball as if they are marking and then supporting the ball out of the circle with the defender. If you want it to be the closest player to the ball, have her call for the ball and the other defenders again, help support the ball out of the circle. In addition, at this time, your goalkeeper should be staying behind the ball as its being taken off of her and then getting up quickly once the defender has the ball. She too should be helping with supporting the ball out of the circle.

chapter 8

Should I Stay or Should I Go?

Working Out Decision-Making Issues

Knowing when to go attack an opponent and when to stay home will come with experience and most likely an older player or coach standing behind them yelling — "GO!" As I've said previously, field hockey is an evolving game so going and not going is not a black and white thing, but I hope some of these will give you a guide so that you can direct your goalkeeper into understanding some of it. The rest will come with experience and learning from others.

What to Do for a Breakaway in Zone 1?

Your goalkeeper will have to learn to see the attacker, the ball, recovering teammates, and the potential as to where the ball could go. As the attacker reaches the 25-yard line and there is no defense close enough to play the ball, the goalkeeper will need to advance with controlled quick steps to the attacker. It is important that these steps are controlled. You do not want the goalkeeper to over run the attacker in this situation. The goalkeeper wants to advance to cut down the angle for the attacker and be able to force the attacker wide of the goalmouth. As the goalkeeper advances, she needs to be aware of where the attacker's head is in relation to the ball. Is she looking down at the ball, or is she looking up with control on the ball?

If the attacker is looking down at the ball, then the goalkeeper can perform a skill and expect to win every time. Remember that to perform a skill, she needs to have the proper engaging distance.

If the attacker is looking up and has complete control of the ball, have your goalkeeper shadow and stay behind the ball in the proper engaging distance. Her objective is to try to slow the attacker's movements down until her defense can recover and help. Remember to have your goalkeeper line her body up with the ball and not the attacker. If the attacker moves off her line, meaning she pulls and gets slightly ahead of the goalkeeper, now is the time for the goalkeeper to perform a skill and attack the opponent.

This concept is used for shootouts too. Use some of the shootout drills to help with this but add a recovering defender and another attacker. If you add another attacker and defender into the breakaway situation, your goalkeeper now has to evaluate more than just the attacking opponent. This type of drill is great for decision-making for your goalkeeper and also for communicating with the defense. Every goalkeeper should be so familiar with their defense that she knows which player can handle which situation.

Try different variations in the center of the field heading towards goal and working specifically on your defense and goalkeeper. Have your goalkeeper do the majority of the communicating and your backfield responding. Then add three attackers with two defenders and then maybe add a recovering defender. Each variation adds new decisions for your goalkeeper and defense. It also gets her more familiar with her defensive players. The more time she spends with her defense the better she knows who has the speed to move to the ball fastest, who responds to her the best, who can handle two players and who can't. Sometimes, your goalkeeper can be so in tune with her defenders that she doesn't have to give too much direction. So the more she gets to play with them, the better the unit should get.

Drill

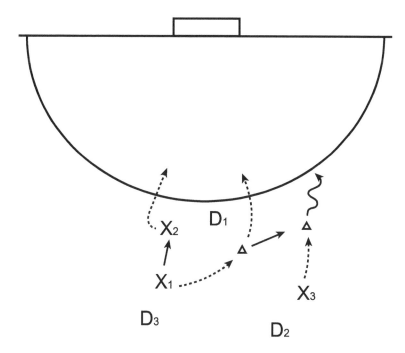

Figure 88: Have X1 start with the ball and pass to X2 who then passes back to X1 at the cone that she cuts to receive on the move. D1 moves to engage and keeps X1 from turning into the center of the field. X1 spins out and then passes to X3 who cuts to receive the ball at the cone and then takes the ball into the circle. X2 and X1 move into the circle once they pass the ball. When X3 starts her sprint to receive the pass from X1, D2 counts "1 Mississippi, 2 Mississippi" and sprints to cover X3. D1 is still trying to keep the ball outside. D1 and D3 have to decide who is taking the ball. Have your goalkeeper direct here and the defense needs to respond. Correct your goalkeeper if she isn't doing what you want for your coaching philosophy. D3 recovers to circle once X3 receives the ball. Play out the ball fully.

They Are Attacking Your Goalkeeper's 45 Angle

Zone 2 (goalkeeper's 45 angle) attackers are extremely dangerous. They get less aggressiveness from the goalkeeper and their angles to cage are more various. Plus remember what I said in Chapter 3 about angles, the 45s for some reason are a weak point for most goalkeepers. If the attacker moves into this area, have your goalkeeper stay poised and patient. Keep in mind the drills that we did earlier in the book. If you have been working these angles, your goalkeeper should be just fine. The first thing your goalkeeper needs to do is move into position so that the angle is correct and then read the attacker and the situation. As I mentioned previously, does the attacker have her head down or does she have control of the ball and sight of the field in front of her?

If the attacker has her head down and she is alone encourage your goalkeeper to advance like she would for a Zone 1 attacker and perform a skill.

If the attacker is alone and has control of the ball and sight of the field have your goalkeeper be patient moving along her angle and watching to react to a shot. By staying along the angle and waiting for a shot, the goalkeeper is increasing her opportunity to react to the shot. Most shots from the Zone 2 will be towards the opposite post that the goalkeeper is moving towards, so by increasing some distance between herself and the attacker, the goalkeeper is giving herself a higher chance of making a very difficult save in this situation.

If the attacker is advancing with others in Zone 2, regardless of head down or up, I tell my goalkeepers to stay home, be patient, move along their angle and react. Of course, this changes according to coaching philosophy but since this area is a weak spot for most goalkeepers, I like them to have the time to react to the ball and make a save rather than advance and get beat.

If the attacker is advancing with others in Zone 2 and there are recovering defenders, the goalkeeper now needs to give very concise direction. "Jane take ball, defense drop and mark." Again, very direct as to who she wants playing the ball. This helps her to not have to worry so much about the other attackers because she knows that they are being marked. She now can focus on the ball. She then can tell Jane "I'm with you," "time," "out," etc. It is important to note that your goalkeeper should be seeing with her peripherals if the other attackers are marked. I tell my goalkeepers that they should not be taking their eyes off the ball to see if her defense is doing their job. This is why I stress the peripheral drills in the earlier chapter on angles.

Drill

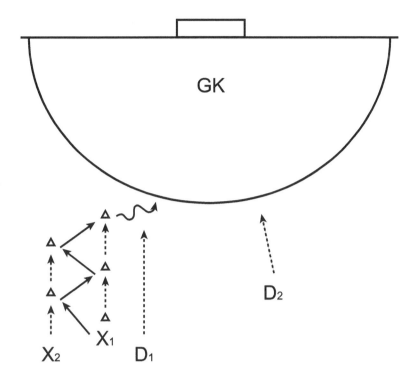

Figure 89: A) This will help lead into figure B. X1 starts with the ball and passes it to X2. At this time D1 and D2 recover. X2 sprints to the cone and receives the pass on the move and passes back to X1 at the next cone. X1 sprints to the cone to receive and passes the ball back to X2 at the next cone. X2 sprints to the next cone. X2 receives the pass in front of the cone and sends the ball back to X1 at the last cone. Here you can have X1 either receive in front of the cone as if cutting off the pass and have her turn into Zone 2 of the circle or you can have her receive before the cone and spin out to take the ball into Zone 2 of the circle. X2 sprints into the circle for support for X1 to try to tip or be a low option pass. X1 engages D1 or D2 depending on the run and what the goalkeeper asks of the defenders. X1 then tries to shoot in Zone 2.

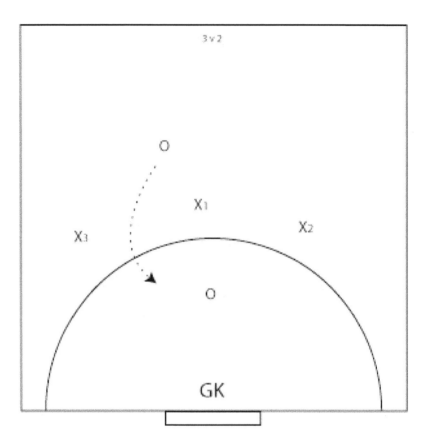

Figure 88: B) This drill will help to give more freedom to the Xs and Ds and make it harder for the goalkeeper to make decisions on what she wants for her defense in open play. X1 and X2 move into the circle once they pass the ball. Set up a game of three versus two toward goal, with three Xs outside the circle and one defender (O) in the circle. Position your other defender (O) up field with the Xs. This defender will be recovering. Have your goalkeeper work on positioning defenders and communication during play.

Endline Attackers – Look Out!

As we all know, Zone 3 does not have much of an angle for a shot. Most attackers in Zone 3 will be setting up shots and passing to Zone 1 or 2 for the shot. You need to make sure your goalkeeper can move quickly through her angles from post to stroke to opposite post. Zone 3 attackers usually bring the ball along the endline and pass it in to an attacker in Zone 2 or Zone 1. Zone 3 may not look dangerous, but with the right attacker — it can be. First let's focus on Zone 3 itself. If your goalkeeper doesn't stick to the post or moves to anticipate a pass and opens up the post, the ball can squeak in for a goal. Besides the 5-hole (between the legs), I think these are the worst goals to get scored on – very embarrassing because they can be easily saved.

The goalkeeper should position herself against the post closest to the ball and make sure that there is no gap between her legs and the post. She should hold her ground and the post until the time is right to move or execute a skill. When making a kick, try to have her use the outside leg for a kick to ensure that there is no gap between the post and your goalkeeper. Have your goalkeeper keep her eyes on the ball and use her peripheral vision to see the rest of the field.

Zone 3 is tough because the goalkeeper has to stick her ground until the last minute and really has to be aggressive and patient at the same time. I mark a spot on the field for my goalkeepers that indicates to them when to advance on an attacker driving the endline and when to stick the post. Again, this will come with experience and a little humiliation to know when and why she will need to perform a skill. I also think that this will come from your coaching philosophy as well. Some coaches are more aggressive and want them to advance and others want their goalkeepers to stay home no matter what. My philosophy is somewhere in between these two.

Left Side of the Field: Endline Attackers

I tell my goalkeepers to advance if the attacker does not have full control and is at the 5-yard hash. I usually have them attack with a slide tackle here on their stick side blocking a pass. I also teach them to go in a v-position to keep the ball from popping up to Zone 2. If the attacker seems to have control of the ball and depending on what the goalkeeper's peripherals see in Zone 2 or 1, I tell my goalkeeper to hold and try to intercept a pass to Zone 2 or 1. Your goalkeeper will need to know how far out she can reach with her stick dive to know what she can intercept or not. If she cannot intercept, her first move should be one step back along her goalmouth to square herself out to make a save across the goalmouth on the line. If she has time to shift up towards the shot after squaring out then that's great. She already knows she's on angle because of her movements. Again, this is why I have them do their angles blindfolded. No looking around to see if she is on angle and it's an automatic muscle-motor memory movement.

If for some reason your goalkeeper goes out to an attacker at the 5 yard hash and gets beat, your goalkeeper needs to get up and dive back across the goalmouth. Another reason why we focus on diving. This is what I call the desperation dive.

Drill

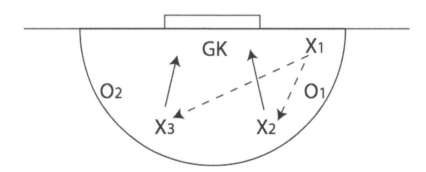

Figure 90: X1 starts on the end-line inside the circle and passes to X2 or X3. X2 or X3 shoots on goal. The goalkeeper must clear to O1 or O2. To vary the drill have X1 dribble into the circle and pass to X2 or X3, or have X2 and X3 run in for a tip or to catch the rebound off the other attacker's shot.

Right Side of the Field: Endline Attackers

I treat this side a little different for my goalkeepers. Again, it's a coaching philosophy and not a black and white thing. I have my goalkeepers stay home unless they see a true opening to play the attacker. Maybe my defense is a step behind the attacker and my goalkeeper needs to come in to double team and prevent the pass. This would be a legitimate reason to advance. Also, remember, I teach my goalkeeper to advance on the opposite slide tackle here (see Chapter 5). However, for the most part, I ask my goalkeeper to hold and let her defense do the work. The defense is on their stick side and should be successful here. I have my goalkeeper focus on the ball and the possible pass.

Drill

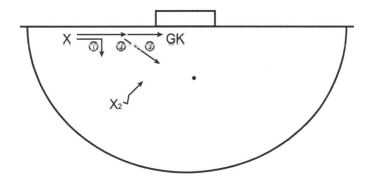

Figure 91: Have your goalkeeper start on the post facing the sideline. X should start just outside the corner hash on the end-line. Do this in three phases for your goalkeeper. X dribbles toward the cage and then turns for an L pass to X2. X2 shoots. This will teach your goalkeeper to drop step on her angle and position herself in Zone 2 and ready for a shot from X2. The second part is to have X dribble the ball in towards the cage and along the end-line. When she gets just about inside the 5-yard hash have her send it to the stroke. Your goalkeeper is to read this pass and stick dive to try to intercept the pass. If she can't intercept, have her drop step and follow the position of the ball. A bonus to this is to add an X3 to the stroke mark to receive the pass and shoot on the goalkeeper. The last phase is to have X dribble all the way in to the goalkeeper. Have your goalkeeper advance when the field player is about 2-3 yards from her and slide tackle X.

The three zones are all handled in different ways. As you can see, your goalkeeper has alot of decisions to make within seconds to prevent the ball from going into the goal. Alot of pressure is placed on the goalkeeper to execute a skill when the ball is shot on goal. Keep that in mind when teaching your goalkeeper and when instructing your team about your goalkeeper.

Now that your goalkeeper understands her role and has grasped positioning and angles in the circle, you can teach her what skills she may need to execute to clear the ball from the circle or attacker.

chapter 9

Communication — What Did You Say?

In my opinion, technical skills are easy to teach a goalkeeper and with a few tweaks here and there, your goalkeeper can improve greatly with her technical skills. However, I find that teaching a goalkeeper what to say is very difficult. Difficult, because, every situation calls for something different. There is no black and white answer like in the technical skill part of the position. Alot of it, comes from knowledge by watching and listening to other goalkeepers or from playing other sports, and, of course, from years of experience of the game. I find it extremely disheartening that most coaches do not at least give their goalkeepers direction on what they should and shouldn't say. By the time they get to me at the college level, I have to correct my goalkeepers and it takes at least a year to fix the communication skills. The majority of goalkeepers are asked by their coaches to talk but are not given the direction as to how. So what I most often hear is "Good job, Jane," etc. I try to tell my goalkeepers that cheering isn't necessary. That's for the sideline and the fans. Of course, some circumstances deserve a good cheer on the field, but for the most part, your goalkeeper should be only giving direction. What her defense needs to know is "Are you behind me and working with me?" or "Are you handling another player?" What specifically does your goalkeeper see? Is there someone who is not marked and can we pull an open defense player on them? These things all have factors as to how well your team will play in the backfield. The goalkeeper is the last line of defense so she has the best view of the field. All communication should be direct, concise, consistent, and don't forget loud.

Your goalkeeper needs to be clear and firm with communication to her defense. It is the goalkeeper's job to keep the team composed and ready for every situation. Composure and effective communication during the game can reduce stress, confusion, and goals allowed. If your goalkeeper is a cheerleader, get her to stop by teaching her the proper things to convey to the team. If your goalkeeper just cheers then the defense learns to tune her out and they won't hear her when she has an important direction to convey later. Let's first start with what terms should be said according to where the ball is located.

Ball Is Above the 50

The goalkeeper should be moving with the ball and focused on the play. By paying attention to the play, she will be able to predict two to three plays ahead which will help her when the ball ends up in her end of the field. All this helps with experience. When the ball is this far away from the goalkeeper, there is no use in talking to the offense. They can't hear her and by the time she gives direction, it's too late. What your goalkeeper can do is watch the opposing forwards and where they are in relation to her defenders. She can also direct the defense in positioning depending on how your team plays. Some teams like to have a deep defender and others don't. If your goalkeeper sees that her defender is sinking too close to her and not with the play to help out the rest of the team on the other end, your goalkeeper can direct her defense to push up and away from her and get involved in the play.

Ball Is Below 50 but Before the 25

When the ball is in this area of the field, your goalkeeper needs to be more focused and anticipating the side of the field that the ball is going to be on when it comes to her end. She can be a little relaxed in her stance but should be more vocal then when the ball was on the other side of the field. She should begin to direct her defense to contain the ball to the right or left side of the field with simple words like "Keep her left" or "right." Some goalkeepers tell their defenders to "Step left" or "right" according to where they want the ball. The terminology or how it is said is up to the team and the coach. Additional things that your goalkeeper can say is whether or not there is an offender creeping in to the circle or if someone isn't marked below the 25-yard line. The last thing, I teach my goalkeeper to do is to try to identify who is the best choice to take the ball based on the situation. This will come with some experience. But if there is a breakaway, your goalkeeper will need to direct a specific defender to take the ball and another to keep dropping, etc. This will come from practice. Have your goalkeeper watch other sports to help understand this. Soccer and ice hockey are two good ones to watch to understand stepping up and dropping back on defense. Again, you want to emphasize to your goalkeeper to not cheer for her teammates at this time. She should be directing their movements on how they approach and defend the ball. Once the defense has come up with the ball, your goalkeeper can also direct where the best pass would be with direction, "See Jane through," etc. Again, these need to be quick, concise, and loud statements.

As a rule of thumb, I tell my goalkeeper to say their directions three times. I have found that sometimes my defense gets so intense that the first direction is a little muddled to them. So they really don't hear the goalkeeper until the second or third statement. Therefore, it would sound like "Keep it right, keep it right, keep it right." The goalkeeper is sure then that the defense has heard it and should be reacting to the statement with short adjustments in their steps. Even if her midfield didn't hear it, you can be certain that the backfield heard it and will relay it up to the midfield. That is if you taught your backfield to communicate to the rest of the team like you have your goalkeeper.

Lastly, I would tell your goalkeeper that once that ball hits about the 30-yard line (just above the 25), she needs to get down in her stance and be ready for anything to happen. The ball will move quickly once it comes in that area and she needs to be ready to react.

Ball Is Inside the 25

Once the ball is inside the 25, your goalkeeper needs to be fully intense and down in her stance ready for anything to happen. Directions should be shorter and more direct, "Jane, mark #1," etc. You want your goalkeeper to pick a side that she wants the ball to be kept to. Try to teach your defense to stick to what your goalkeeper is requesting. Even if it's wrong, I'd rather see that my defense is listening and responding to my goalkeeper than not. It's easier to fix how your goalkeeper gives the direction than to teach your team to trust and do what your goalkeeper is requesting.

As a simple rule of thumb, I tell my goalkeeper that if the ball is coming down the middle, she should have the defense force it out to the right of the field. If it's on the right, keep it there. If it's on the left keep it there. However, this changes according to your coaching philosophy. Some coaches always (well about 90% of the time) want the ball forced to the right. Why? Because it's your offenders weak side and your defender's strong side. You'll have to decide what your philosophy is and communicate that to the team. I've always had a strong backfield on both the right and left sides so I am not concerned if we force it to our nonstick side. I trust my defense to handle the ball and, if they don't, I trust my goalkeeper to get the job done. So you will have to decide for yourself if my rule of thumb is right for your team depending on your philosophy and team personnel.

Since ball movement gets faster at around the 25-yard line, your goalkeeper will need to be very precise with what she wants. She will need to focus not only on the ball and her defense but also her opponent's movement. That's why I say that your best player should be your goalkeeper. She must be able to remain calm, make quick decisions, and be able to play the ball under pressure. Your goalkeeper must be able to make decisions in a split second and possibly change that decision when the situation changes. She must be able to instantly think of her next move while executing the current move.

Every team uses different terminology for movement in the defensive end. However, some of these terms still remain used across the majority of teams. So while your goalkeeper is moving around and concentrating on the ball, she will also need to use terminology similar to these:

Pressure	I'm behind	Out	Coming on
Hard right/left	Take	Mine	Cover
Force right/left	Stay mark	Go	Bring her
Mark	Keep her	Drop	Go to ball
Time	Outside left/right	Shift	Crossing
Up top/stroke	Shot	Switch	Let

Ball Is Inside the Circle

Emphasize to your goalkeeper that the circle is her domain and she has to take charge of it. The goalkeeper is the leader of the circle and the defense must work with her to prevent a goal. A good goalkeeper will be able to read the game, direct defense, and position herself. A goalkeeper should be able to focus on and see all areas of the field, even the area that is behind her. It takes skill and practice to be able to move, direct defense, watch the play, and anticipate passes and moves of the attacker. That is why I emphasize that your goalkeeper should know her angles so well that she can do it blindfolded. It has to be an instinctual muscle-motor memory for her. In addition, as you saw in the drill under the angles chapter, I work their peripheral vision as well so that it becomes a natural part of her movements.

Once the ball enters the circle your goalkeeper should get shorter with her direction and say much less because she has to focus on the ball and possible shots coming her way. I tell my goalkeeper to keep it to the important things, like moving defense onto a player quickly if need be, and where to force the ball or bring the opponent into herself, etc. At this point, the direction is really only given once or twice. Once she sees that the attacker is about to shoot she should call for the ball. I have my goalkeeper's say "shot" so that my defense is aware it's coming and that my goalkeeper has it. Please make sure that when your goalkeeper calls for the ball with a "mine" or "shot" statement that your defense does not reach in to intercept. You need to allow your goalkeeper to play that ball. She is set for the ball to come at her at a specific angle and ready to play it. If her defender reaches in, she could tip the ball into the cage or allow the shot to be deflected at an angle your goalkeeper was not set for. These types of goals are extremely upsetting and can cause arguments with the backfield and goalkeeper. Work with your defense to make sure that they play their mark and are ready for a pass or to prevent their mark from tipping the shot without reaching in to intercept the shot. This will mean you will need to do a lot of circle-type play drills to work your defense and goalkeeper on all types of situations.

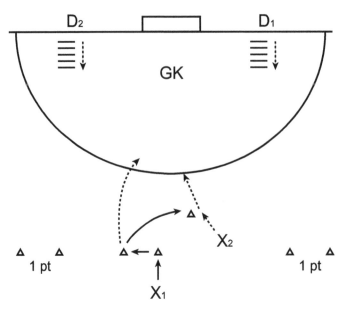

Figure 92: *Although this is more of a 2v2 drill, I like it because it not only works conditioning, it also works communication. Place ladders out at the edge of either ends of the circle. Have your defense behind the end-line just behind the ladders. X1 starts with the ball on the whistle and dribbles to the cones and pulls left and around the cone. Then X1 passes to X2. X2 cuts to receive the ball and take it into the circle. X1 cuts into the circle. Meanwhile, the 2 Ds on either end must run through the ladder and organize themselves to play defense. The goalkeeper needs to choose the person in the best position to take the ball and which way to force the ball. This is a great drill to work all ends of the circle. You can enhance this drill by giving defense and attack points. Create gates for your defense to work the ball to. If they make it to the gates with support, they get 1 point. If the attack scores or gets a corner, they get 1 point. You can also add a target for your goalkeeper and if they clear to the target they get 1 point.*

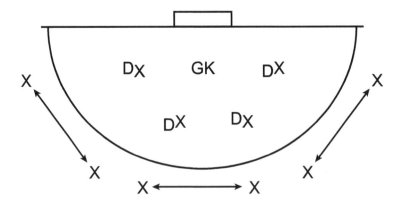

Figure 93: *Xs on the outside pass a ball back and forth with each other. Work one area at a time. Place 4 attackers and 4 defenders in the circle. Have them moving as the ball is being passed around. When the passing Xs see an opening, they can try to penetrate with a dribble or pass the ball to an X inside the circle. Then play the ball out fully.*

Now that we know when to use certain terms, etc., let's define what some of these words or terminology mean so that you can see what fits best in your philosophy of defense. The majority of these terms can also be used by your field players too.

Pressure or Go to Ball — The goalkeeper is asking the defender to step and play the ball. The goalkeeper may see that there is too much cushion between the ball and the defender.

Go or Take her — The goalkeeper is seeing an opening in the play and she wants the defender to urgently attack the ball to keep it from progressing forward.

Coming On — The goalkeeper is telling a defender that there is someone coming on to attack her from behind.

Bring Her or Keep Her Coming — The goalkeeper sees that there is an opportunity to double team and is asking the defender to bring the attacker into the goalkeepers feet.

Force Right/Left or Keep Her right/left — The goalkeeper is asking the defenders to position themselves to keep the ball from crossing the center of the field and keep the ball to one side of the field so that the goalkeeper has less of the cage and only 2 angle areas to worry about. To keep it simple, some coaches just tell their goalkeepers to say "keep it outside or force outside"

Drop — The goalkeeper wants other defenders to drop back and get in position to mark and play the ball coming in the circle.

I'm Behind — The goalkeeper wants the defender to know that she is there for help. Usually a lead in to the double team.

Mark* — The goalkeeper sees that there is an open player. If possible, the goalkeeper should use a defender's name and the offender's number to help with this direction.

Stay Mark — The goalkeeper sees that the defenders are drifting off their marks or she is about to attempt a skill and wants them to stay where they are and hold their positions to clear the path for her.

Up Top or Coming In Up Top — The goalkeeper sees that there is an open player entering the circle in the most dangerous shooting spot of the field, top of the circle.

---

*Mark is defined as an attacker inside the circle who the defender is responsible for defending and making sure that they do not receive the ball.

Endline — This term can be used for several instances, it will depend on what your goalkeeper puts after it as to what it means. For instance, if she says "endline coming in," she is saying there is an open player on the endline moving into the tipping position. She wants her defenders to position themselves to cover a pass to the player moving into the tipping position. If she says "bring her endline," she wants the defender to contain the player along the endline thereby almost forcing her out of bounds.

Cover Stroke — The goalkeeper sees that there is an attacker not marked on the stroke mark or she is anticipating a pass to the stroke. She wants a defender to play this area to cover a danger the goalkeeper anticipates.

Cover — The goalkeeper wants the defender to drop behind them to cover the passing lane. This is used in a pressure cover situation where the goalkeeper is playing the ball.

Crossing In Front or Behind — The goalkeeper sees an attacker crossing in front or behind her or a defender. She can use this direction when the ball is anywhere on the field. This will help deep defenders when the ball is on the offensive end or when the ball is in the circle. She will need to finish the statement with "me or you". To be more specific she could say "crossing behind Jane." Meaning, "Jane, there is a player that is running behind you to your other side. Be ready for a pass to her."

Shift — The goalkeeper is asking the defenders to shift in their marks and movements as the ball moves from one side of the field to the other. This happens when the ball moves across the top of the circle from one side to the other.

Switch — This should be used mainly by defenders communicating with themselves about switching their marks. Occasionally a goalkeeper will ask for a defender to come off her mark and cover the goalkeeper's mark so that the goalkeeper can step up to play the ball.

Out — This is used in two different ways. One is to remind the defenders that the ball should be carried out of the circle to the outside. The other is to tell the defenders that the goalkeeper is on her angle and sees that the ball is going wide of the cage.

Let — The goalkeeper sees that the ball is going wide of the cage or is shot outside the circle and is asking the defenders to let it go and not touch it.

Outside Left/Right or Hard Right/Left — The goalkeeper is telling her defenders that she wants the ball out of the circle on one side of the field or the other. Due to urgency she can add "hard" to it to tell the defenders to hit it instead of carry it out. It will depend on what the goalkeeper sees. In addition, she can also add a teammate's name that she wants the ball to be hit or carried to. You can also use "outside left or right" instead of saying "force."

Time — The goalkeeper is telling the defender that there is no attacker coming on them and they have time to move with the ball before passing.

Mine or Shot or I Go — The goalkeeper is calling for the ball and doesn't want her defenders to play the ball. "I go" is used often for when a goalkeeper is flying on a corner. I mainly only hear "I go" in indoor play.

Any one of the above directions should be followed by a defender's name.

chapter 10

Specialty Skills

If you work on fixing the other skills in this book, your goalkeeper will be ready to handle the specialty skills of corners, strokes, and shootouts. All three of these skills and many others can be handled with the other skills talked about in this book.

Shootouts

Shootouts are new to the scene of field hockey but they do make the game more exciting and personally fairer at finding an outcome. Because they are crucial to the outcome of a game, they need to be practiced not only by your field players but also by your goalkeeper. The stick dives and slide tackles are used most often in these scenarios. Have your goalkeeper work on her stick dives from Chapter 7 and from *Mastering the Net*. These will help. When it comes to shootouts, it's really about the engaging distance and a race against the clock. As I mentioned before, have your goalkeeper perform her skill a stick to a stick-and-a-half-length away from the ball. Have her aim solely for the ball and be lined up with the ball not the player. In shootouts it's extremely important that your goalkeeper attacks on the front 45 angle. She wants to keep the ball out in front of her. She only has to hold off her opponent for 8 seconds, so if she keeps the ball in front and away from the cage, she will win the shootout. I tell my goalkeeper that she is competing against the clock in shootouts. If she can control her opponent for the allotted time then she will be successful.

Drills

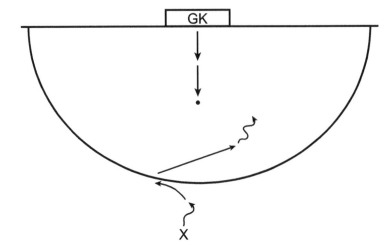

Figure 94: Start with an attacker on the 25-yard line with a ball and the goalkeeper on the endline in the center of the goalmouth. Start with X just going straight at your goalkeeper and have her react like she learned in slide tackles in the earlier chapter. Then have X dribble left then dribble right to engage the goalkeeper. Have your goalkeeper react to that movement. Then again, have X dribble right and then dribble left to engage the goalkeeper. Work different scenarios out with your goalkeeper and work on her weak points with engaging and winning a shootout. Remember, it's about beating the clock with shootouts.

Corners

Penalty corners are so difficult to teach because the philosophy changes according to the coach, the personnel, style of defense, field surface, and level of play. I have worked in all levels and on all different types of field surfaces and my philosophy always changes on corners. There is not a hard fast design for corners and goalkeeping. However, if you have worked on all the other areas of goalkeeping that we discussed in this book, your goalkeeper will be ready for anything when it comes to corners. There are some areas that can be worked for "outside the box" ideas in this area though.

Where Should My Goalkeeper Start?

Too often I see goalkeepers starting in all sorts of positions during corners. Some stand upright, and some are on the post or even hidden behind field players. I even see fliers crossing in front of goalkeepers and blocking the goalkeeper's runs. The one person that you want in the correct position and ready for a shot is your goalkeeper. She is your last line of defense and should be the first one that is set and ready for a shot. The best method to successfully save a ball during a corner for a goalkeeper, is to have her start in the center. With that said, your defensive "flier" should always be to your goalkeeper's left.

So, have your goalkeeper start in the center of the cage no matter what side of the cage the ball is being inserted. This is very similar to her angle runs that she practices in earlier chapters so it should be a very comfortable run for her. Most likely from this position, your goalkeeper will be lined up with the top shooters at the top of the circle, thereby making this a straight run for her and covering her angles correctly should the ball go to the top of the circle. In addition, if the ball comes out to a low angle, again, it's a straight run to where the ball is going and along her angles.

Before the corner begins, I tell my goalkeeper to wait just one step in front of the goal line on the field until the entire team is ready inside the cage. I tell her to face out towards the opponents but turn her head to watch her defense. When her defense says they are ready, then I tell her to take one step back into the cage in her starting position.

Lastly, have your goalkeeper start in a runner's stance, with one foot forward and one foot back. Which foot she chooses is based upon which foot is dominant and most natural for her. From here her first motion forward should be to bring the back foot forward and across the goal--line as quick as possible. Try to cut out any stutter stepping here, because every second counts. It should be one quick, smooth motion forward. If your goalkeeper struggles with this, talk to your track coach or even a strength and conditioning coach.

Figure 95: An example of where a goalkeeper should be positioned in the center of the cage.

If Your Goalkeeper Lies Down

If your goalkeeper lies down for corners, then you will need to work on her wrist strength, leg scissors, and balls at the belly for bouncing balls.

Drills

This drill is for a goalkeeper that lies down on corners. Sometimes there is a freaky ball that will bounce over the stick hand or a banana ball over the legs. You will need to practice these with your goalkeeper. Have your goalkeeper lie in her normal position for a corner. Place a small ramp at the stick hand. Have someone at the top of the circle hit a ball at the ramp and have your goalkeeper flick her wrist to catch the ball on the lift off the ramp to keep in front of her. This will take some wrist strength. Similarly, move this ramp to the belly for the glove hand to practice and to the feet for the top leg to practice the scissor.*

Figure 96: This is an example of a ramp in use.

---

*Scissor legs is when the top leg slices up in the air to prevent a bounced ball from bouncing over the legs.

If Your Goalkeeper Stands Up

If your goalkeeper stands up on corners, there are some balls that can be practiced.

Drills

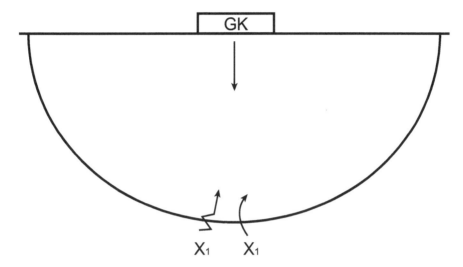

Figure 97: Start with a pile of balls at the top of the circle. Have two people up there, one hitting balls and one to throw balls. Have your goalkeeper start behind the line as if there is a corner. Have them run out like there is a corner happening. The hitter will count to two or three and then hit the ball at the goalkeeper. When the goalkeeper makes the save, have the second feeder throw a ball at the goalkeeper. The second feeder can lob the toss, bounce it or roll it. This will work multiple shots at once. A variation of this would be to start with a toss like a drag flick and then have a shooter on the sides to send additional shots.

Quicker Reactions for Blinded Balls

I occasionally get calls from friends and coaches saying that they need help with their goalkeeper on blinded balls. They tell me their goalkeeper is good at everything else, but once there is a scramble in the circle and there are too many bodies, she loses sight of the ball and is seconds behind to make the save. It is hard to simulate these conditions in your practice, so you will need to work them in your goalkeeper's warm-up.

Drills

Have your goalkeeper set up in her basic stance in her home position just below the stroke mark. You should be behind her with a pile of balls. Roll or toss balls from behind your goalkeeper out in front of her. Keep her with her back to you. As soon as she sees the ball, she is to run on to it and clear it to a target. Don't forget to work the right and the left side of your goalkeeper. This drill will lead you into more complicated blinded drills. Think of ways you can work something like this in for your goalkeeper while playing with the team in circle play. Keeping your goalkeeper scanning the field if she has a problem with these types of plays will help her reaction get faster and she will be more aware of attacker player movement and how she will know where the ball is even though she can't actually see it.

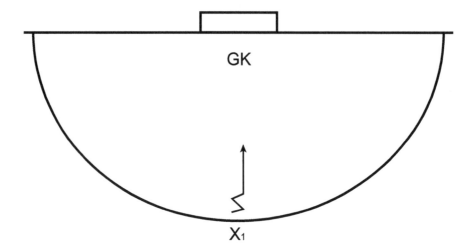

Figure 98: Have your goalkeeper start with her back to the attacker. Have the attacker at the top of the circle with a pile of balls. You should be able to do about 8-10 repetitions of this. The attacker yells "turn" and hits the ball to the cage. At that moment your goalkeeper will turn and try to find the ball. It should almost be at her feet at that point. Once she finds the ball and tracks it, she is to clear the ball. Most of the time these are reactionary clears but you can still put targets for them to aim for. Something that is achievable by opening up the hip and foot correctly on the reaction. You can move the attacker around but try to focus on one side of the circle at a time.

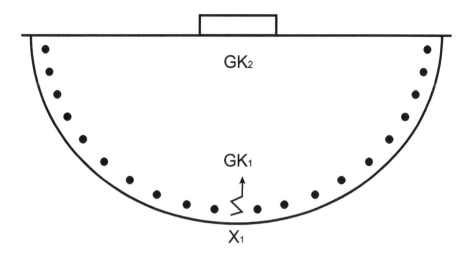

Figure 99: You will need two goalkeepers for this drill. So if you have the luxury of having more than one goalkeeper on your team, this is a great way to incorporate them. Place balls all around the circle line. Have your attacker choose which ball she would like to focus on. Place your spare goalkeeper directly in front, about 1 foot away from the attacker and the ball. Her back should be to the cage and the GK2. GK2, should be set up and ready to clear a ball coming from X. GK1 should position herself so that GK2 cannot see the ball at all. GK2 can move GK1 into a position to cover the ball if GK2 can see it. X will say "jump" and hit the ball. GK1 will jump either in a straddle or by pulling her feet up to her rear-end so that the ball can travel underneath her. Timing is important here. It is important that the ball travel underneath GK1 and that X hits it hard at GK2 so that GK2 gets the simulation of a game-like hit. GK2 won't see the ball until it is coming out from under GK1 so it will work quick reaction skills for your goalkeeper and how to play a ball that you can't totally see but you have an idea of where it is.

The last drill you could put together for blinded balls is to go to your local toy store and purchase some punch dummys. These are the things that fill with water at the bottom and air on the top and when you hit them they bounce back upright. Scatter these all over your circle. Now create a drill around them. Dribble behind them and then shoot coming out a side, etc. It will simulate circle play and bodies being in the circle for your goalkeeper without using players.

Defense

Let's talk real quick about defense around the goalkeeper during a corner. Where they stand is up to your coaching philosophy, but where they start is important. As I mention, the "flier" should always be to the left of the goalkeeper no matter which side of the field the ball is inserted. The goalkeeper and the flier are almost fighting for the center position in the cage. You want the flier next to the goalkeeper almost as close as she can get without affecting each other's run out of the cage. It would be very dangerous if they tripped each other up on the way out of the cage. Whether you like your right trail on the inside or outside of the cage, she should always be positioned to the right of the goalkeeper and giving her some space. Don't have her on top of the goalkeeper. I like to position my right trail with her hip against the post so that she knows where it is on her run out of the cage. With that in mind, the left trail positions herself the same way but on the left post. The last player is the post player. This position is always tricky. This position is based on where the ball is being inserted. She should position herself to the left of the goalkeeper directly behind the left trail (if the trail is inside the cage) if the ball is being inserted on the traditional side of the field. If the ball is being inserted on the nontraditional side, I have my post position herself to the right of the goalkeeper directly behind the right trail (if the trail is inside the cage). Again, in general this may change based on your coaching philosophy but the one thing I would not change would be where the flier starts. Figure 100 should give you an examples of what the start should be for these positions.

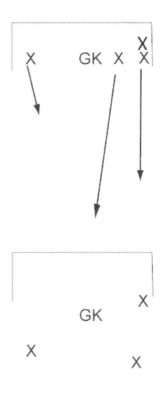

Figure 100: Here is where your defense and your goalkeeper should be standing inside the cage. Remember, the goalkeeper should always start in the center of the cage with her flier to her left. Trails and post players can be anywhere based on your coaching philosophy, however, I personally like them inside the cage unless I know something special about an opponent. The second part of this figure shows where your players should run (again based on my philosophy) when the ball is inserted for a standard corner setup. Obviously there are different types of corners and how defense can exit the cage. You will need to refer to another reference for advanced corner setups. This is just a reference for a basic corner defense setup.

chapter 11

Saving the Stroke!

A penalty stroke is awarded when the defense commits a foul that prevents a probable goal. The skill of strokes is a dying art. Strokes are highly debated and have recently no longer been a highlighted skill to learn. Since this skill is not used often anymore, you barely see teams practice them on a regular basis. Since shootouts determine tie games now, strokes are becoming more obsolete. Nevertheless, they still are a part of the game and something every goalkeeper needs to learn how to perform properly. Your goalkeeper should have this skill in her repertoire and it should be practiced so that the outcome of your game can be changed.

Think about if your goalkeeper has never practiced this skill and this is the deciding factor of the game. It could be seconds left of the game and the score is zero versus zero. If your goalkeeper is not prepared to stop this ball by not having practiced strokes with the team, it could mean a loss. Or vice versa if your field player has not practiced. I work this with my goalkeepers several ways. First you want to get her focusing on the correct things – the ball only. The next thing is you want your goalkeeper to always go with her hands out to the ball. The last things are balance, distance and proper landing.

Strokes are used like a penalty kick in soccer. It is called when a foul occurred by the defense to prevent a sure goal. The ball is placed on the stroke mark and your goalkeeper needs to stand still on the line until the ball moves. *Mastering the Net* can give you the basics on how to perform a stroke. Pay close attention to the landing for penalty strokes. This is the only instance in which a goalkeeper can almost roll onto her back in the field of play. This type of landing saves the body from injury.

There are a few things with strokes that need to be pointed out. I've noticed that with strokes almost every goalkeeper has some fear. Goalkeepers will get on the line and get themselves psyched up and ready to take on that attacker, but for some reason as the ball comes to them, they barely move to the ball. I've seen it across all age ranges of goalkeepers.

So start your goalkeeper like you did for the stick dives in a safety crouch dive position, etc. Then work your way up to the basic stance. As you see in *Mastering the Net*, you want your goalkeeper to place her head behind the ball and the palms of her hands facing the ball. She wants to aim for the ball to hit her chest for there to be a solid block and safely redirect the ball. Keep repeating to your goalkeeper, head and hands first. Her legs may be longer, but her hands will be faster. Every save she makes for strokes must be done with her hands and positioning the head, hands, and chest behind the ball. Every movement will come out of her core and push the ball out and away from the goal.

Stroke diving should not be attempted until she knows how to properly dive from previous chapters. In addition, teaching her how to properly land from *Mastering the Net* is important too because it takes less pressure off the shoulder, elbow, and ribs during the landing. Start small and easy with mats on either side of the cage when practicing several strokes or dives in a row to save your goalkeeper's body from being beaten up.

Strokes

Focus on the Ball

Many goalkeepers feel that it helps them to look at the stick and the feet to see what direction the ball is going in, but unfortunately, looking at these things can inhibit her ability to stop the ball. So you can do several things to help on the focus.

Drills

Mark a spot on the ball (large x or dot). Have this spot face your goalkeeper and have your goalkeeper focus on the spot during strokes. Add adjustments to this and have the stroker do funny things with her feet before she strokes.

Another suggestion, is to have your goalkeeper look at the ground until she hears the whistle, then she can look up, find the ball, and react. I had to do this for one of my goalkeepers once because she had an issue with staring at the ball too long and it froze her up for reactions. So, we worked on quicker reactions to the ball and focusing on the ground then looking up to find the ball. She was actually very successful in the cage with this little tweak.

Go with Hands

If you look at the chapter on diving, there should be some drills in there that should help with this as well. For some reason, goalkeepers have a problem in strokes because they refuse to try to catch the ball or allow their feet to leave the ground. Some of these drills should help to get some air between the ground and your goalkeeper. First thing you need to tell your goalkeeper is that she should try to catch the ball with her chest behind her. Use for example a softball/baseball catcher. You see the majority of the time a catcher makes a catch, it's done with her chest behind the ball. The chest creates a large amount of surface area to keep the ball in front. Also if I tell my goalkeeper to aim for her chest to catch the ball, she gets more distance in her dives to the ball. For strokes, you will want your goalkeeper to go out towards the ball and not be diving into the post. Let's work some drills emphasizing these two concepts.

Figure 101: An example of how the goalkeeper should be diving out towards the ball and not into the post. You want your goalkeeper to get distance past the post so she will need to be out in front it on her dive.

Drill

Work one specific area at a time. I take the band that I use for kicking and put it on my goalkeeper, then I replace the glove with a garden glove. I use tennis balls and toss them to the designated area and ask my goalkeeper to catch the tennis ball. It's extremely difficult to catch the tennis ball with only one hand while moving and the band and other things are in the way, however, the concept should be there for them.

Did they get a hand on it? Did they redirect it, deflect it, something? So long as they are always going with their hands for this area, remove the garden glove and band and have them put the proper equipment on. Use a field hockey ball and toss again to the area you are focusing on. You should see an increased improvement. When you feel confident enough with your goalkeeper being able to retrieve the tosses, perform a real stroke working on specific areas again.

Drills

First start with your goalkeeper on her knees with no stick or gloves and a mat on either side of her body. The mat helps for when you are doing multiple diving exercises. It not only softens the blow to the body but it also gives the goalkeeper more confidence to dive and land because the mat is there. Use a soccer ball or football and send tosses to either side of the goalkeeper. Have your goalkeeper aim for her hands and chest to get behind the ball and have her fall on the mat. Work both sides of the body. Then gradually work your way up the safety crouch, again, working both sides of the body. The last step is to get them into their basic stance. Again, we still want them catching the ball with their chest behind the ball. Move the mats to just outside the post. Continue with tosses to either side of the body. You can work one side then the other too. You will want your goalkeeper to aim for the mat just outside the goal post while catching the ball.

You need to make sure that you work all areas of the goal cage for strokes. Many of us call this "around the world." You will need a skilled stroker for this or you can do tosses, but most goalkeepers like to see it come off a stick and have a true motion for visuals. Have your goalkeeper setup for a stroke in her basic stance and the ball at the stroke mark. Start with a roll to them (directly down the middle). They need to drop into a stack (slide tackle without the sliding forward part) and protect the cage keeping the ball in front. Then work your way with tosses or scoops to the right slowly moving up towards the head. When you get to the head, send one directly over the goalkeeper's head. She should react by directing it back out or up and over the cage. Then continue in a clockwise direction over to the left of the goalkeeper and back down to her feet. This works all areas of the goalmouth.

Balance, Distance, and Proper Landing

For more information on these three refer to *Mastering the Net: Field Hockey Goalkeeping Basics.*

Drills

This drill will work on getting the distance you want for your goalkeeper on strokes. Have your goalkeeper set up for a stroke and attach a resistance band (from previous drills) to her waist. Have the stroker and goalkeeper set up for a stroke and an assistant on the side of the cage creating resistance on the cord. Have your goalkeeper dive to save the ball, and the assistant that is on the resistance cord should move with the goalkeeper so that she can dive to the ball. Do this a few times then take off the resistance band and do the drill again. You should see more distance with the dive. Obviously, you are only working one side at a time.

This drill will work on getting the distance you want for your goalkeeper on strokes. Have your goalkeeper set up for a stroke and put a marker where the right foot is placed on the line. Have your goalkeeper dive to save the ball to the left. Mark where that right foot lands and show her the distance. Have her try to increase this distance with every dive. Obviously, you are only working one side at a time.

Figure 102: Use your bungee resistance cord for this drill. Have your goalkeeper in her basic stance on the goal line. A coach will be on the other end of the bungee giving your goalkeeper resistance to the side of the cage. A player will be at the stroke mark and will be sending strokes to a specific area of the cage. Focus on one side at a time. Have your goalkeeper extend and reach for the ball, trying to come in contact with the ball with her chest. Remember always going with hands to the ball. The coach will add some resistance to the aerial extension that your goalkeeper is trying to perform and slowly give and release with the goalkeeper so that your goalkeeper can land properly. I actually just walk forward with the goalkeeper so that she can perform the skill but I'm adding resistance to her the entire time she is trying to come in contact with the ball. Do this several times then take the bungee off and let your goalkeeper perform the skill on her own without resistance. Notice the distance your goalkeeper now gets with her extension to the ball. You should use resistance training once a week so that your goalkeeper gets stronger and is more capable of extending farther out to come in contact with the ball.

Final Notes on Strokes

The last thing to note about strokes is that, you want to make sure your goalkeeper is only looking at the ball. She should follow the ball all the way in to her hands and push out of her core, then deflect the ball out of the cage. If you see your goalkeeper move one direction when the ball goes the other, she most likely was watching the stick or feet of the attacker. For purposes of the stroke, she needs to solely focus on the ball. Attackers know all kinds of tricks to fool the goalkeeper into going the wrong direction. Remind her to follow the ball into her hands and out of the goal.

chapter 12

Peripheral Vision

Did I Just See What I Thought I Saw?

What is peripheral vision? Well, it is all that is visible to the eye outside the central area of focus, otherwise known as side vision. Did you know that goalkeepers and field players should be using it in the field of play? No one really talks about peripheral vision in goalkeeping. I occasionally will hear some coaches discuss it to their players when they talk about field vision. Peripheral vision is not totally an essential piece to learn for a goalkeeper. I find it more useful than essential. If knowledge is power then peripheral vision will help a goalkeeper gain more knowledge on the field and thus more power. I focus on this with higher level goalkeepers so that they can use it to scan the field quickly while focusing on the ball. First see how far each goalkeeper's peripheral vision goes. If your goalkeeper wears glasses or contacts, her peripheral vision may not be as good as someone who doesn't. But that doesn't mean she shouldn't use it. Practicing peripheral vision is the easy part but putting it into the field of play is more difficult.

Drills

Have your goalkeeper start in her basic stance at a cone. Stand off to her side and about 2-3 feet away from her vertically and horizontally. Make her sprint up to a cone about 5-7 yards away. Hold up a colored cone. Ask your goalkeeper to backpedal to the start cone and while still facing forward (without turning her head), have her tell you what color cone you are holding up. Make sure she says it loud and as quickly as she sees it. From here you will see how far her peripheral vision range is. Do this a few times alternating different-colored cones. Make sure you do the right and left side of your goalkeeper. As a bonus to this drill, create a shot coming to her at the top cone so that she has to clear and then move backward again.

Remember when you were a kid and you used to put your hands out to a friend and she would put her hands out underneath yours? You would stare into each other's eyes and try to psych each other out. Then your friend who was on the bottom would try to move her hand up and slap your hands on the top. Although you thought this game was silly and a way to pass the time, it's actually a great way to work peripheral vision with your goalkeeper. If you have two goalkeepers, take a few minutes and play this game.

Another game is to take two tennis balls and place them in each of your hands. Hold your arms out at shoulder width apart. Have your goalkeeper in her basic stance and facing you close enough so that she can catch the tennis ball if you drop it. Look at each other's eyes and when the time feels right drop a tennis ball. First start with your goalkeeper catching it with both hands. Then work your way up to right hand only, left hand only, opposite hand only, etc. It's a fun game for you and your goalkeeper and it works quick reaction skills along with peripheral vision.

You can always build peripheral vision in your drills. If you are doing drills with cones and footwork, have your goalkeeper move through a cone series with backpedals and when she sees the cone in her peripheral she can explode to a forward cone. Anything you can do to work her peripheral vision in a drill will help your goalkeeper later when she needs to see the field without having to turn her head.

When to Use?

Since we practice peripheral vision, I know that my goalkeeper has it and understands why we practice it. I tell her specific times I want her to use it on the field to give her a guide. One time to use it is when she is moving along her angles as the ball is moving along the inside of the circle. She uses her peripheral to see if there is an obstacle in her way and to make sure she is in line with the post on her movement. The other time she can use it is to see if a player is marked. She can glance while focusing on the ball and notice colors. If she doesn't see her team color with the opponent's color then she can direct her defense to pick up the loose player to her right or left, etc. I mention to her that she will not be able to see clear direct numbers but she will see blobs of colors and she will be able to determine how many blobs of colors and if there is danger in one area versus another. This is why I can't emphasize enough the importance of reversible pinnies at practice. If you want your goalkeeper to be able to not only identify right in front of her, where the threat is and who isn't covered, etc., as well as the ones in her peripheral vision, color differences between attack and defense are important. This peripheral vision skill comes with tons of practice and knowledge of the game as well as near perfection on the other skills and decision-making.

chapter 13

Conclusion

Share Your "Outside the Box" Ideas

Goalkeeping is not an easy position. Not only does your goalkeeper need to focus on her skills and executing them correctly, but she also needs to direct her defense and be aware of everything that is happening on the field. And to top that all off, she has to be willing to change her mind quickly due to what is happening on the field. Someone once told me that goalkeeping is 90% mental and 10% physical. If you work with your goalkeeper and give her the skills and confidence to perform those skills, the 10% will kick-in and help your team succeed. It is all about confidence in the goal and your goalkeeper will not be confident if she isn't sure of the skill. Thinking "outside the box" with your teaching will help her get better and tweak the bad habits, mistakes, poor decision-making, etc., so that she will be more successful in the goal. The more successful she becomes the more confident and less mental but more instinctual the game will be for her.

As your goalkeeper develops, you will need to work on her multi-tasking and peripheral vision. Keep your goalkeeper active in aspects of play while you work with your field players. She will need to learn how each position works so that she can direct them more efficiently or know how to defend against them. Keep in mind the more knowledge that she has about each position, the better she will be in the goal for you. Your goalkeeper will always be learning because field hockey is an evolving game. As equipment changes and rules change, we as coaches have to adapt and evolve as well with our teachings. As new equipment comes out, more thinking "outside the box" ideas will have to come in play to help goalkeepers adjust to a new type of rebound or altering their body to perform a skill the proper way. Think about new ways to teach your goalkeeper besides just sending her a ball and asking her to kick it out of the circle at a target.

If your goalkeeper is struggling with something, turn to other coaches from other sports for ideas. They can help tremendously on giving you some "outside the box" ideas for new drills. Please share these ideas with the community. Chances are, one of us has come across an athlete in our coaching years that needed help on that same thing and could use your drill for it. We, as a sport in the US, can only get our goalkeepers better if we share and collaborate with each other. As I said, it's hard enough to do all the things goalkeepers are asked to do, so sharing ideas will definitely help the position. I hope that this book has helped you with some ideas for drills and ways to tweak or strengthen their skills. Good luck and remember, any idea you have that is "outside the box" is worth a try to see if it will work to help your goalkeeper succeed.

Appendix

I have included some drills that are helpful for your team and your goalkeeper. There are some footwork drills and some team drills here. Remember that when you are working these drills with your team, there are certain things you need to emphasize for your goalkeeper. Before each drill, review what you would like your goalkeeper to focus on.

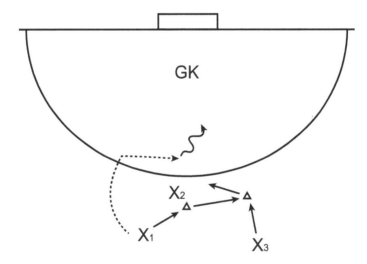

Figure 1: X starts with the ball and sends it to X2 at the cone. Then X1 runs to the top of the circle. I like to make this an L cut. X2 cuts up to the cone to receive the ball from X1. Then X2 passes to X3 at the cone. X3 cuts onto the ball and receives it from X2 at the cone. She then passes to X1 who has now timed her L cut to receive the pass from X3 and shoots.

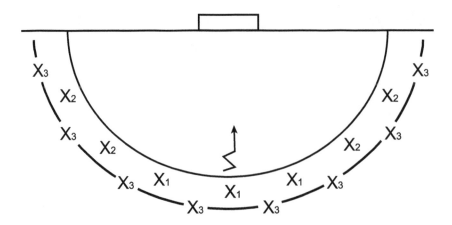

Figure 2: Place all your players around the circle and on the dotted line. Only X1s can run in to the circle to play the rebound. The ball can come from either X1s or X2s. After the ball has been shot, X1s can rush to retrieve the rebound off of the goalkeeper. X3s can then move up onto the circle and should be filling in the gaps. The purpose of this drill is to keep the ball in the circle. Award one point to the goalkeeper for making clears outside the circle. If the Xs score they get a point. Try to limit the scrambles to no more than 3 and then the ball is dead. This can be a fun game but it is a full workout for your goalkeeper.

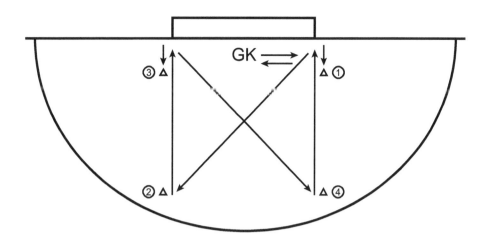

Figure 3: This is another footwork drill that you can do for your goalkeeper to keep it fresh to work their angles. I like to call this the star drill. Have your goalkeeper start in the center of the cage on the goalmouth and shuffle to the post and face out to the sideline. Then have her shuffle to cone 1. At cone 1, have her then drop step and sprint to cone 2. Then drop step and sprint to the post. Then shuffle to cone 3. At cone 3, have her drop step and sprint to cone 4. Then drop step and sprint to the post. To end have her drop step at the post and shuffle back to the center of the cage where she started.

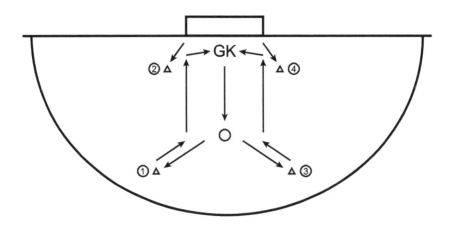

Figure 4: This is another footwork drill that I like to use to work the skills of my goalkeepers. I call this "working my area". Have your goalkeeper start on the goalmouth in the center of the cage. Have her sprint to the stroke mark and then turn and sprint to cone 1. As she approaches cone 1 have her slide tackle it. Then have her get up and sprint back to the post. At the post have her stick dive out to cone 2, then get up and do a desperation dive across the goalmouth. It is important that your goalkeeper keep her chest facing out to the field for this dive. Make sure that she doesn't turn her back to do the dive. Then have her get up and work the other side. Have her sprint to the stroke mark and then turn and sprint to cone 3. As she approaches cone 3 have her slide tackle it. Then have her get up and sprint back to the post. At the post have her stick dive out to cone 4, then get up and do a desperation dive across the goalmouth.

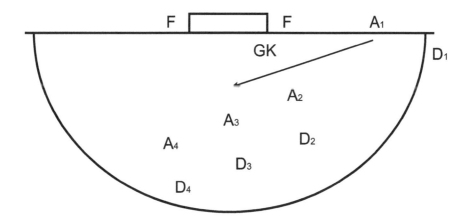

Figure 5: A1 starts with the ball. Fs have a pile of balls and stand behind the end-line. Ds are to stand 3 feet behind the As. Whistle is blown and A1 sends a cross ball (one that is out of the reach of the goalkeeper). A2, 3, and 4 are to retrieve and try to deflect in. They should be moving towards the cage in almost a wave once the whistle is blown to receive this cross ball. Ds are working to keep the As from retrieving the ball. Once the coach deems the ball dead (by going over the endline, outside the circle, or a foul) then either F can send in a ball from the endline. Try to catch your goalkeeper off guard. This should not be a pass to the As. It should be more a loose ball kind of play in the circle. After that ball is dead, the other F then sends in a ball from her side to be played.

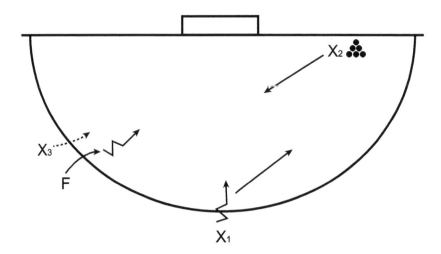

Figure 6: This drill will work shots from several different areas. X1 starts with the ball and shoots. X1 then sends a ball to X2 who sprints to receive and shoots. X2 then sprints to a pile of balls behind her and passes one to stroke for X1 to run on and try to score. Then F sends in a bouncy ball into the circle and X3 hits it on the bounce to the cage. It is up to you if you want X1 and/or X2 to play rebounds in this drill. In addition, you can alter this drill by having X3 pull back and put the ball in the air on her own and then catch it on the bounce. You could place an obstacle there for her to pop the ball over and then try to catch the ball on the bounce. There are many ways you can alter this drill to work for you.

Lightning Source UK Ltd.
Milton Keynes UK
UKHW032017191118
332619UK00010B/646/P

9 781930 546233